My Heart Sings Out

COMPILED AND EDITED BY

FIONA VIDAL-WHITE

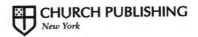
CHURCH PUBLISHING
New York

Musical autography by Music Graphics International

Church Publishing Incorporated
Permissions
445 Fifth Avenue
New York NY 10016

Every effort has been made to trace the owner or holder of each copyright. If any rights have been inadvertently infringed upon the Publisher ask that the omission be excused and agree to make the necessary corrections in subsequent editions.

Copyright notices appear at the end of each selection. Copyright holder addresses are listed beginning on page 246.

10 9 8 7 6 5 4 3 2 1

INTRODUCTION

All my life as a church musician, I have gravitated towards working with children. As a teenaged chorister, I wrote folk songs for my friends in youth group and short choruses for worship services. My first church music post was as director of a Saturday arts workshop funded by the Church of England's Church Urban Fund, which centered on singing with children, using the kind of repertoire this hymnal brings together.

When I came to the United States in 1992, I saw the challenges of finding good church music for children. The few materials available often had inadequate texts with poor theology and overly simple tunes. As a Children's Music Director, I worked with clergy and educators. I collected excellent music which often included songs from different cultures, and I began giving workshops on how to teach them. My parish started an inter-generational worship service, and I refined the materials and methods we had developed.

For this collection, I have surveyed many sources of music for congregations of all ages as well as mainline denominational and children's hymnals, probably more than 3,000 pieces in all, to compile music that dates from 1980 onwards. My primary concern has been to acknowledge that many children do not become fluent hymn-readers (that is, those who can both read and sing unfamiliar words laid out under a melody), until about the age of ten – which is exactly when their interest in attending church is rapidly eroding. These young children are, however, excellent memorizers of both music and words; therefore, many songs in this collection use short repetitive texts. Those with longer texts are chosen for their repetitive structure and story-telling qualities. Hymns in traditional form must have a chorus or repeated phrase that will engage this age group.

Each selection was made with attention to the highest standards of musical, lyrical and theological quality. The over-arching style of this music is variously called "contemporary," "ethnic," "popular," or "modern." One of the goals for *My Heart Sings Out* is to show that this style is appropriate and accessible for use in church when care is taken to find compositions of quality. Knowing that the children will not get to sing the music if adults don't enjoy it too, I have included songs and hymns that are most effectively sung in harmony unaccompanied. Not all churches have organs and organists today, and this music encourages strong congregational singing and individual competence. Even more importantly, there is a theological message to be learned when we sing together: as each of us offers the gift we have together, we create something of great beauty and mystery.

This book is essentially liturgical. It is arranged according to the shape of the liturgy and the church year. It will be invaluable for inter-generational liturgies. Indexes will help you find songs appropriate to the season, occasion or festival, and their place in the liturgy.

My Heart Sings Out is also useful for those planning church school, children's chapel, and vacation church school programs. This music will enliven your Sunday worship and your educational programs. Children will develop a repertoire that will accompany their faith journey throughout life, and adults will discover the gift of their singing voices and the joy of sharing this music as a family.

Fiona Vidal-White

TABLE OF CONTENTS

Come, Holy Spirit

Cantor

Come, Ho - ly Spi - rit.

Come, Ho - ly Spi - rit,

Come, Ho - ly Spi - rit.

Come, Ho - ly Spi - rit.

Ma - ra - na - tha!

Ma - ra - na - tha!

Come, Lord, come.

Come, Lord, come.

*When repeated, hold this note through beginning cantor part.

Uyai mose *Come all you people*

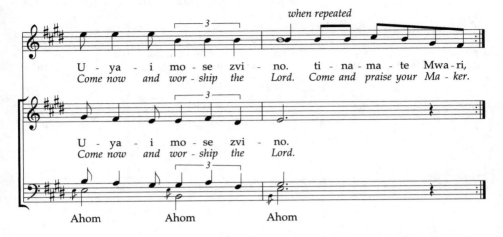

when repeated

U - ya - i mo - se zvi - no. ti - na - ma - te Mwa - ri,
Come now and wor - ship the Lord. Come and praise your Ma - ker.

U - ya - i mo - se zvi - no.
Come now and wor - ship the Lord.

Ahom   Ahom   Ahom

Come into God's presence 3

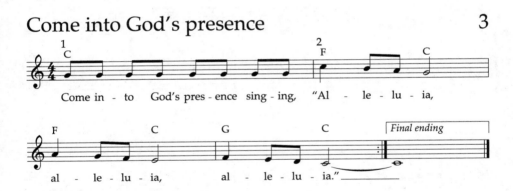

Come in - to God's pres - ence sing - ing, "Al - le - lu - ia,

al - le - lu - ia, al - le - lu - ia."

Final ending

Additional verses may be added: Come into God's presence singing, "Worthy the Lamb . . ." Come into God's presence singing, "We love you so . . ." Come into God's presence singing, "Glory to God . . ." Come into God's presence singing, "Jesus is Lord . . ."

Dios está aquí *God is here today*

Dios es - tá a - quí,_____ tan
God is here to - day:_____ as

cier-to co-mo el ai - re que res - pi - ro,_____ tan
cer - tain as the air I breathe,_____ as

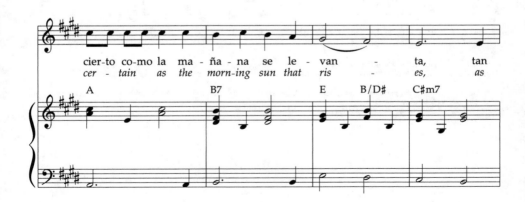

cier-to co-mo la ma - ña - na se le - van - ta, tan
cer - tain as the morn-ing sun that ris - es, as

cier-to co-mo que le can-to y me pue-de o - ír._____
cer - tain when I sing you'll hear my song._____

Words and Music: Mexican, tr. C. Michael Hawn, 1998; arr. C. Michael Hawn and Arturo Gonzales, 1999
© 1999 Choristers Guild, 2834 West Kingsley Road, Garland, TX 75041-2498 [www.choristersguild.org].
All rights reserved. Used by permission.

Glory to God

Glo - ry to God _____ in _____ the high -

est, _____ and _____ peace to God's peo - ple on

earth. _____ to God's peo - ple on earth. _____

Lord_____ God, heav - en - ly King, al - might - y God and Fa - ther, we wor - ship you, we give you thanks, we_____

praise you for your glo - ry.

Glo - ry to God in the high -

est, and peace to God's peo - ple on

earth. _____ to God's peo-ple on earth. _____

Lord Je - sus Christ, on - ly Son of the Fa - ther, Lord _____

God, Lamb of God, you take a - way the sin of the

world: have____ mer - cy on____ us; you are

seat - ed at the right hand of the Fa - ther: re -

ceive our____ prayer.____

For you a - lone are the Ho - ly One, you a - lone are the Lord, you a -

lone are the Most High, Je - sus Christ, with the Ho - ly Spir - it, in the

glo - ry of God the_____ Fa - ther._____

Glo - ry to God_____ in__ the high - est.

A - men, a - - men._____

The congregation may sing only this repeated section when a cantor or choir sings the full text.

Glory to God

♩. = 76

Glo-ry to God in the high - est, and

peace to his peo-ple on earth.___ Lord God, hea-ven-ly King, al-

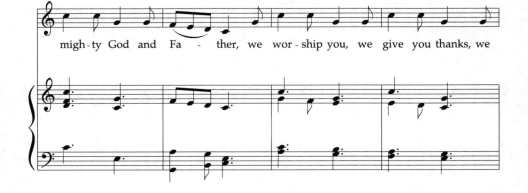

migh-ty God and Fa - ther, we wor-ship you, we give you thanks, we

praise you for your glo - ry.

♩ = 60

Lord Je - sus Christ, on - ly Son of the Fa - ther, Lord God,

Lamb of God, you take a - way the sin of the world: have

Lord, ____ you a - lone are the Most High, Je - sus

Christ, with the Ho - ly Spi - rit, in the glo - ry of God the

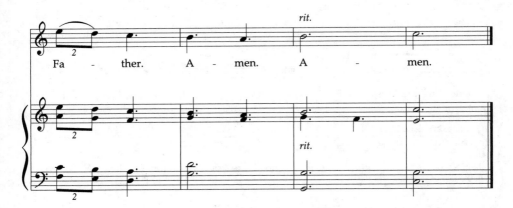

Fa - ther. A - men. A - men.

Glory to God

Glo - ry to God in the high-est, peace ____ to his peo-ple on earth.

Lord God hea-ven-ly King, al - might-y God and Fa-ther, we wor-ship you, we

give you thanks, we praise you for your glo - ry. Lord Je - sus Christ,

on - ly Son of the Fa - ther, Lord God, Lamb of God, you take a -

way the sin of the world; have mer - cy on us; you are

seat-ed at the right hand of the Fa - ther; re - ceive our prayer. For

you ____ are the Ho - ly One, you ____ are the Lord, you a -

lone are the Most High, Je - sus Christ, with the Ho - ly Spi - rit, in the

glo - ry, the glo - ry, the glo - ry of God the Fa-ther. A - men.

Words: from The Book of Common Prayer (1979) of the Episcopal Church USA.
Music: Jonathan Dimmock (b. 1957), from *Missa Appalachia* © 2002 Jonathan Dimmock.
All rights reserved. Used by permission.

Give thanks to the Lord our God

Rendei graças ao Senhor

Give thanks to the Lord our God for our God is good, ver - y good,
Ren - dei gra-ças ao Se - nhor, por-que e - le é bom, e - le é bom;

for God's lov - ing kind-ness lasts for - ev - er and for - ev - er. Oh
por que su-a mise-ri-cór - dia, du-ra pa-ra sem-pre pa - ra sem-pre. Ben-

bless-ed, bless-ed be our God; God of Is-ra - el, now and for - ev - er.
di - to se - ja o Se - nhor, De-us de Is-ra - el de e - ter - ni - da - de

Let all the peo-ple say A - men, al - le - lu - ia!__
e to-do o po - vo di - qa A - men,

al - le - lu - ia,__ al - le - lu - ia,__ al - le - lu - ia!__

Gloria, gloria

*Refrain

1
Glo - ri - a, glo - ri - a, in ex - cel - sis De - o!

Dm Gm C F Dm Gm C F

3
Glo - ri - a, glo - ri - a, al - le - lu - ia, al - le - lu - ia!

Dm Gm C F Dm Gm C F

Verses
Cantor

1 Glo - ry to God in the high - est,____ and

peace to his peo - ple on earth.

Lord God, heav-en - ly King, al - might-y God and Fa - ther,___ we

Refrain ad lib.

wor - ship you, we give you thanks, we praise you__ for your glo - ry.__

2 Lord Je - sus Christ, on - ly Son of the Fa - ther,__

Lord God, Lamb of God, you take a - way the sin of the world:

have mer - cy on us; you are seat - ed__ at the right hand

Refrain ad lib.

__ of the Fa - ther:__ re - ceive our prayer. __ 3 (For)

you a - lone are the Ho - ly One, you a - lone are the Lord,

you a - lone are the Most High, Je - sus Christ,

with the Ho - ly Spir - it, in the glo - ry of God the Fa - ther.

To refrain

A - men, a - men, a - men, a - men!

* The refrain may be sung as an ostinato throughout all or part of the text, or it may be sung as a response at the beginning and after each section of the text.

Words: from The Book of Common Prayer (1979) of the Episcopal Church USA.
Music: Jacques Berthier (1923-1994) © GIA Publications, Inc., 7404 S. Mason Ave., Chicago, IL 60638 [www.giamusic.com]. All rights reserved.
Used by permission. *You must contact GIA Publications, Inc. to reproduce this music.*

10

I thank you, Jesus

11
Glory to God

Lord, have mercy

Cantor Lord,____ have mer - cy. *All* Lord,____ have mer - cy.

Cantor Christ,____ have mer - cy, *All* Christ,____ have mer - cy.

Cantor Lord,____ have mer - cy on us, *All* Lord,____ have mer - cy on us.

May be sung throughout by congregation.

Kyrie eleison

Ky - ri - e e - le - i - son.____ Ky - ri - e e - le - i - son.____ Ky - ri -
Chri - ste e - le - i - son.____ Chri - ste e - le - i - son.____ Chri -

e e - le - i - son.____ Ky - ri - e e - le - i - son!____
ste e - le - i - son.____ Chri - ste e - le - i - son!____

repeat Kyrie

14

Kyrie eleison

Kyrie eleison

15

Ky - ri - e e - lei - son. Chri - ste e - lei - son.

Ky - ri - e e - le - i - son.

Ky - ri - e e - lei - son. Chri - ste e - lei - son.

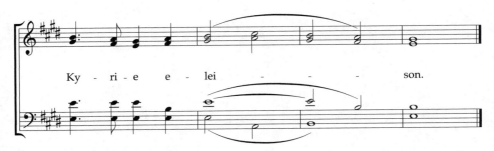

Ky - ri - e e - lei - son.

16

Holy, holy, holy God

Ho - ly, ho - ly, ho - ly God, Ho - ly and Might - y,

Ho - ly and Im - mor - tal, have mer - cy on us.

Holy God

Ho - ly God,   Ho - ly and Might - y,   Ho - ly Im -

mor - tal One, have mer - cy on us.   mer - cy on us.

18

Halle, halle, hallelujah!

Hal - le, hal - le, hal - le - lu - jah!

Hal - le, hal - le, hal - le - lu - jah!
Hal - le - lu - jah!

Hal - le, hal - le, hal - le - lu - jah!

Hal - le - lu - jah! Hal - le - lu - jah!

Words and Melody: Traditional Caribbean. Arr. Mark Sedio (b. 1954) © 1995 Augsburg Fortress, PO Box 1209, Minneapolis, MN 55440-1209 [www. augsburgfortress.org]. All rights reserved. Used by permission.

Hallelujah

Hal - le - lu - jah,_____ hal - le - lu - jah,

Hal - le - lu - jah, hal - le - lu,

Hal - le - lu - jah, hal - le - lu - jah,

hal - le - lu - jah,_____ hal - le - lu - jah!

hal - le - lu - jah, hal - le - lu - jah!

hal - le - lu - jah, hal - le - lu - jah!

Celtic Alleluia

Al - le - lu - ia, al - le -

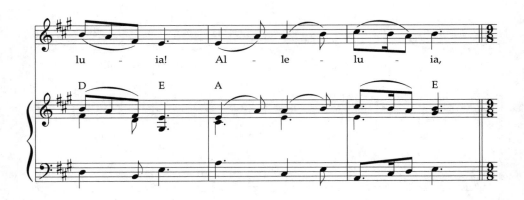

lu - ia! Al - le - lu - ia,

al - le - lu - ia!_____

Allelu, alleluia

Cantor

Al - le - lu, al - le - lu - ia. Al - le - lu, al - le -

Al - le - lu, al - le - lu - ia.

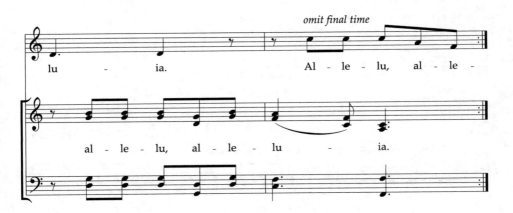

omit final time

lu - ia. Al - le - lu, al - le -

al - le - lu, al - le - lu - ia.

Heleluyan *Alleluia*

He - le - lu - yan, he - le - lu - yan: he - le, he - le - lu — yan;
Al - le - lu - ia, al - le - lu - ia: al - le, al - le - lu - ia;

he - le - lu - yan, he - le - lu - yan: he - le, he - le - lu — yan.
al - le - lu - ia, al - le - lu - ia: al - le, al - le - lu - ia.

* May be sung as a round.

Lord, in your mercy

Lord, in your mer - cy, Lord, in your mer - cy hear our prayer.

Lord, in your mer - cy, your mer - cy, hear our prayer.

Lord, in your mer - cy hear our prayer.

Lord, Lord, hear our prayer.

His love is everlasting

His love,_____ his love,_____ his

love_____ is ev - er - last - ing._____

I will praise your name

I ___ will praise your name for___ ev -

er, my ___ King and my God.

Holy, holy, holy *Santo, santo, santo* 26

"Ho - ly, ho - ly, ho - ly," an - gel hosts are sing - ing.
"San - to, san - to, san - to," can - tan se - ra - fi - nes.

"Ho - ly, ho - ly, ho - ly is the Lord our God.
"San - to, san - to, san - to, Dios es el Se - ñor.

Ho - ly, ho - ly, ho - ly is God, the Lord of might. Your
San - to, san - to, san - to es fuer - te nue - stro Dios. Tu

glo - ry fills the heav - ens, your glo - ry fills the earth." Ho -
glo - ria lle - na los cie - los, la tie - rra lle - na es - tá." Ho -

san - na in the high - est, ho - san - na is our song.
sa - na en las al - tu - ras, ho - sa - na la can - ción.

Words: based on *Isaiah 6:3*, English paraphrase Bert Polman, 1985.
Music: *Merengue*, Spanish; harm. AnnaMae Meyer Bush, 1985 © 1987 CRC Publications, 2850 Kalamazoo Avenue Southeast, Grand Rapids,
MI 49560 [www.crcpublications.org].

Your kingdom come, O Lord

Your king-dom come, O Lord. Your king-dom come, O Lord. _ Your

king-dom come, O Lord. _ Your king-dom come, O Lord.

O bless the Lord

brightly

O my soul, O my

O bless the Lord,_____ O bless the Lord,_____

soul, bless the Lord and ne-ver for-get his

___ O bless the Lord, bless the Lord and ne-ver for-get his

love! O my soul, O my

love! O bless the Lord,_____ O bless the Lord,_____

soul, bless the Lord and ne-ver for-get his love!

___ O, bless the Lord, bless the Lord and ne-ver for-get his love!

God ever-faithful

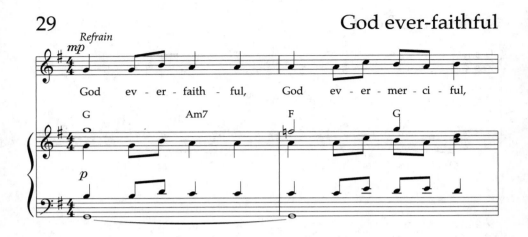

Refrain

mp

God ev-er-faith-ful, God ev-er-mer-ci-ful,

G   Am7   F   G

p

God of your peo - ple, hear our prayer.

Em   Asus4   A   F   C   G

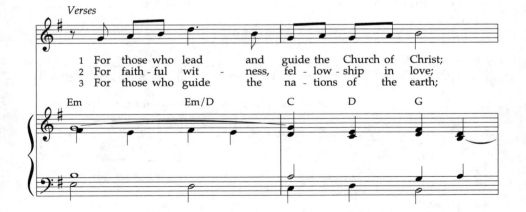

Verses

1 For those who lead and guide the Church of Christ;
2 For faith-ful wit - ness, fel-low-ship in love;
3 For those who guide the na-tions of the earth;

Em   Em/D   C   D   G

for lov - ing care, we pray to you, O Lord:
for liv - ing hope, we pray to you, O Lord:
that wis - dom reign, we pray to you, O Lord:

Am   G/B   A7/C#   D   D.C.

Additional verses

4   For those who seek and serve the common good;
    that justice reign, we pray to you, O Lord:

5   For neighbors' needs, for shelter from the storm;
    for homes of peace, we pray to you, O Lord:

6   For those in sorrow, anguish, and despair;
    that they find hope, we pray to you, O Lord:

7   For those oppressed, for those who live in fear;
    that they be freed, we pray to you, O Lord:

8   For all the sick, the dying, and the dead,
    be life and grace, we pray to you, O Lord:

9   That we might live in peace from day to day;
    that wars will cease, we pray to you, O Lord:

10   That we may stay faithful, open to your Word;
    your Kingdom come! We pray to you, O Lord:

11   For all the dreams held deep within our hearts;
    for all our needs, we pray to you, O Lord:

12   Entrusting all we are into you hands,
    we call your name, and pray to you, O Lord:

Kyrie eleison

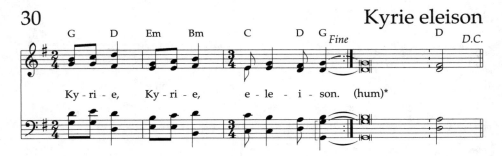

Ky - ri - e, Ky - ri - e, e - le - i - son. (hum)*

Petitions may be sung or spoken here.

Words: from The Book of Common Prayer (1979) of the Episcopal Church USA.
Music: Jacques Berthier (1923-1994) © Les Presses de Taizé (France) (admin. GIA Publications, Inc., 7404 S. Mason Ave., Chicago, IL 60638 [www.giamusic.com].) All rights reserved. Used by permission.
You must contact GIA Publications, Inc. to reproduce this music.

Mungu ni mwema *Know that God is good*

Mu - ngu   ni mwe - ma.   Mu - ngu   ni mwe - ma.
Know that   God is   good.   Know that   God is   good.
Ha - le,   ha - le - lu - ya.   Ha - le,   Ha - le - lu - ya.

Mu - ngu   ni mwe - ma,   ni mwe - ma,   ni mwe - ma.
Know that   God is   good,   God is   good,   God is   good.
Ha - le,   ha - le - lu - ya,   Ha - le - lu - ya,   ha - le - lu - ya.

Words: Traditional.
Music: Democratic Republic of Congo. Source unknown © copyright control. Arr. Edo Bumba © 1997 WGRG The Iona Community (Scotland) (admin. GIA Publications, Inc., 7404 S. Mason Ave., Chicago, IL 60638 [www.giamusic.com].) All rights reserved. Used by permission.
You must contact GIA Publications, Inc. to reproduce this music.

Lord, I pray

32

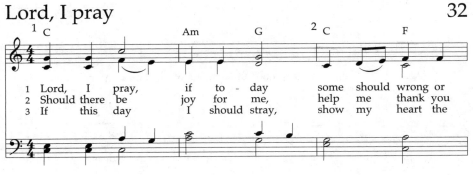

1 Lord, I pray, if to-day some should wrong or
2 Should there be joy for me, help me thank you
3 If this day I should stray, show my heart the

trou - ble me, make me kind; bring to mind
as I should. Let me through all I do
road to take. Should I fear, please be near;

your for - give - ness makes me free.
praise you, Lord, for all things good.
hear my prayer for Je - sus' sake.

This may be sung as a round or canon in two parts.

Words: Jean C. Keegstra-DeBoer, 1949, alt.
Music: Dutch melody, arr. Grace Schwanda © 1983 CRC Publications, 2850 Kalamazoo Avenue Southeast, Grand Rapids, MI 49560 [www.crcpublications.org]. All rights reserved. Used by permission.

Day by day

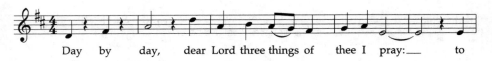

Day by day, dear Lord three things of thee I pray:___ to

see thee more clear - ly, to love thee more dear - ly, and

fol - low thee more near - ly, day by day.

Words: att. Richard of Chichester (1197-1253).
Music: Fiona Vidal-White © 2004 Fiona Vidal-White.
All rights reserved. Used by permission.

Amen, siyakudumisa *Amen, we praise your name* 34

Ma - si - thi: A - men, si - ya - ku - du - mi - sa. Ma - si - thi:
Sing a - men: *A - men,* *we praise your name,O* *God.* *Sing a - men:*

A - men, si - ya - ku - du - mi - sa. Ma - si - thi: A - men, Ba - wo,
A - men, *we praise your name, O* *God.* *Sing a - men:* *A - men,* *Ba - wo,*

A - men, Ba - wo, a - men, si - ya - ku - du - mi - sa. Ma - si - thi:
A - men, *Ba - wo,* *a - men,* *we praise your name. O* *God.* *Sing a - men:*

(not sung final time)

Words and Music: *Masithi*, South African Hymn © 1983 Lumko Institute, PO Box 5058, Delmenville, South Africa
[www.catholic-johannesburg.org.za]. All rights reserved. Used by permission.
Transcr. David Dargie © 1983 Choristers Guild, 2834 W. Kingsley Rd., Garland, TX 75041-2498 [www.choristersguild.org]. All rights reserved. Used
by permission.

35

Thuma mina *Send me, Lord*

Thu - ma mi - na, Thu-ma mi - na, Thu - ma mi - na, Thu-ma
Je - sus,   send   me   Je - sus,   send   me

1.–3.
Send   me   Lord,

4.

mi - na   So - man - dla.
Je - sus,   send   me   Lord.   *Send   me   Lord.*

Additional verses

3 *Call:* Lead me, Lord, *Response:* Lead me, Jesus.
4 *Call:* Fill me, Lord, *Response:* Fill me, Jesus.

Words: South African.
Music: *Thuma mina*, South African © 1984 Walton Music (admin. Licensing Associates, 935 Broad St. #31, Bloomfield, NJ 07003 [www.waltonmusic.com].) All rights reserved. Used by permission.

Holy, holy, holy Lord

Ho - ly, ho - ly, ho - ly, Lord, God of pow-er and

might,_____ hea-ven and earth are full of your glo - ry.

Ho - san - na in the high - est. _____ Bless-ed is the

one who comes in the name of the Lord. Ho - san - na, ho - san - na,

ho - san - na in the high - est, the high - est._____

Holy, holy, holy Lord

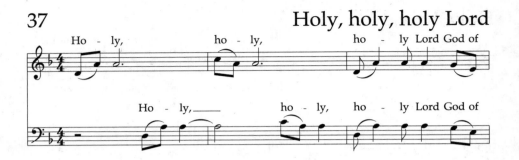

Ho - ly, ho - ly, ho - ly Lord God of

power and might. Heav - en, earth, ____

heav-en and earth are full of your glo - ry. Ho - san-na in the

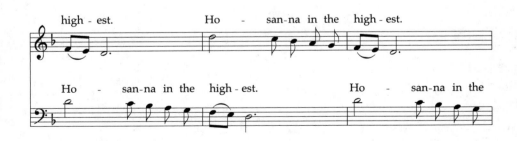

high - est. Ho - san-na in the high - est.

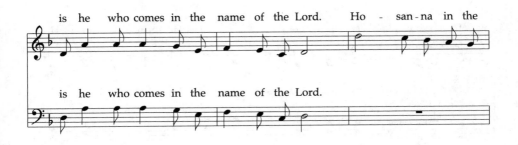

Words: from The Book of Common Prayer (1979) of the Episcopal Church USA.
Music © 1988 WGRG The Iona Community (Scotland) (admin. GIA Publications, Inc., 7404 South Mason Ave., Chicago, IL 60638
[www.giamusic.com].) All rights reserved. Used by permission.
You must contact GIA Publications, Inc. to reproduce this music.

Holy, holy, holy

Holy, ho-ly, ho - ly,___ God of power and

might,____ heaven and earth are full,_____ are full

of___ your glo - ry.___ Ho - san - na! Ho - san - na! Ho -

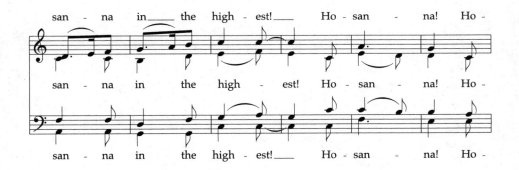

san - na in___ the high - est!___ Ho - san - na! Ho -

Holy, holy, holy Lord

Ho - ly, ho - ly, ho - ly Lord, God of pow-er and might,____

____ hea - ven and earth are full of your glo -

ry.____ Ho - san - na in____ the high-est.

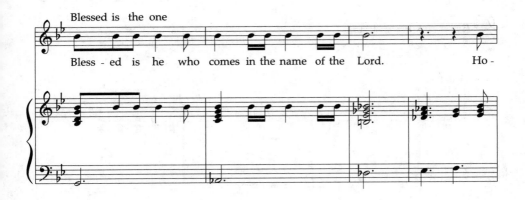

Blessed is the one

Bless - ed is he who comes in the name of the Lord. Ho -

san - na in the high-est.

Words: from The Book of Common Prayer (1979) of the Episcopal Church USA.
Music: Carl MaultsBy, from *The Saint Mary Mass* © 1989 Malted Milk Music, 575 Riverside Drive # 51, New York, NY 10031-8545. All rights
reserved. Used by permission.
You must contact Malted Milk Music to reproduce this music.

Holy, holy, holy Lord

Capo3: (D)
F

Ho - ly, —

ho - ly, — ho - ly Lord, God of pow-er and might,

(G) (D) (A)
Bb F C

heav-en and earth, heav-en and earth are full of your glo - ry..

(D)
F

(G) (D/F#)(Bm) (G) (Em/A)
Bb F/A Dm Bb Gm/C

Words: from The Book of Common Prayer (1979) of the Episcopal Church USA.
Music: Rob Glover (b. 1950), from *Mass of Plenty* © 2000 GIA Publications, Inc., 7404 South Mason Ave., Chicago, IL 60638
[www.giamusic.com]. All rights reserved. Used by permission.
You must contact GIA Publications, Inc. to reproduce this music.

Our Father in heaven

Nossinan* / Our Father in heaven, hal - low'd be your Name,   your kingdom come,

your will be done, on   earth as in hea - ven.   Give us today our dai - ly bread.

Forgive us our sins as we forgive those who sin   a - gainst us.

Save us from the time of tri - al,   and deliver us from e - vil.

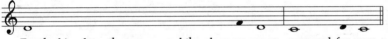

For the kingdom, the power, and the glory are yours, now and for ever.

A - - men.

Ojibway word. Option for "Our Father" pronounced noh-sih-hahn.

Words: from The Book of Common Prayer (1979) of the Episcopal Church USA.
Music: Monte Mason, from *Red Lake Mass* © Monte Mason. All rights reserved. Used by permission.

Our Father in heaven

Our Fath - er _____ in hea - ven, hal - low - ed

be your Name, _____ your king-dom come,

your will be done, on earth as in hea - ven.

Give us to - day our dai - ly bread. For - give us our sins as

Words: from The Book of Common Prayer (1979) of the Episcopal Church USA.
Music: Carl MaultsBy, from *The Saint Mary Mass* © 1989 Malted Milk Music, 575 Riverside Drive # 51, New York, NY 10031-8545. All rights reserved. Used by permission.
You must contact Malted Milk Music to reproduce this music.

O Lamb of God

Cantor or Congregation

O Lamb of God that tak - est a - way the sins of the

world, have mer - cy, have mer - cy on us. _____

S O Lamb of God that tak - est a - way the sins of the

A Oh . . .

T Oh . . .

S world, have mer - cy, have mer - cy on us. _____

A

T

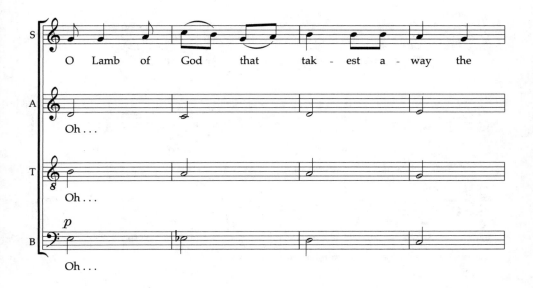

O Lamb of God that tak - est a - way the

Oh . . .

Oh . . .

Oh . . .

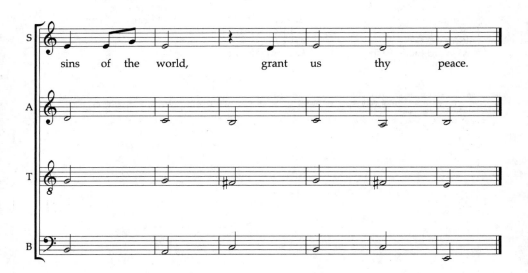

sins of the world, grant us thy peace.

The choral parts may be played by the organ. However, the organ should not play the melody.

Words: from The Book of Common Prayer (1979) of the Episcopal Church USA.
Music: Jonathan Dimmock (b. 1957), from *Missa Appalachia* © 1989 Jonathan Dimmock.
All rights reserved. Used by permission.

O Lamb of God

*Cantor**

**O Lamb of God, you take a - way

Repeat as needed

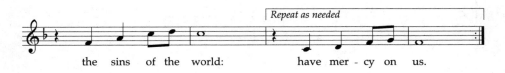

the sins of the world: have mer - cy on us.

Last time

Grant us your peace, grant us your peace.

* *The congregation echoes each phrase of the cantor at the interval of one measure.*

** *Additional Invocations*

Advent
O Morning Star
O Word of God
Emmanuel

Christmas
O Word made flesh
Emmanuel

Lent
O Tree of Life

Easter
O Risen Lord
O Cornerstone
O Spring of Life

General
O Bread of Life
O Cup of Joy
O Prince of Peace

Lamb of God

Lamb of God, you take a-way the

sins of the world:____ have mer-cy on us. Lamb of God, you

take a-way the sins of the world:____ grant us peace.

Take, O take me as I am

Take, O take me as I am; sum-mon out what I shall

be; set your seal up-on my heart and live in me.

Words and Music: John L. Bell (b. 1949) © 1994 WGRG The Iona Community (Scotland) (admin. GIA Publications, Inc., 7404 South Mason Ave., Chicago, IL 60638 [www.giamusic.com].)

Behold, I make all things new

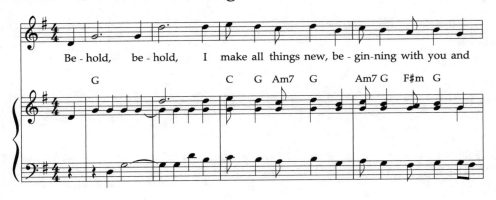

Be - hold, be - hold, I make all things new, be - gin-ning with you and

G | C G Am7 G | Am7 G F#m G

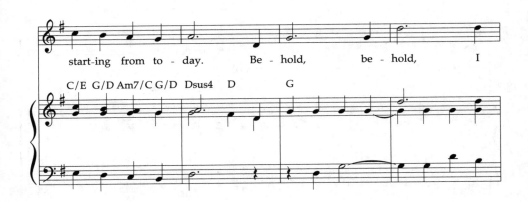

start-ing from to - day. Be - hold, be - hold, I

C/E G/D Am7/C G/D Dsus4 D | G

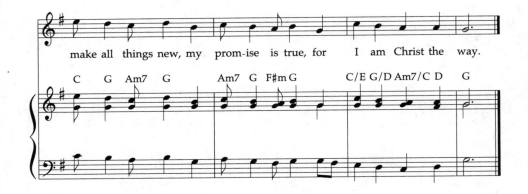

make all things new, my prom-ise is true, for I am Christ the way.

C G Am7 G | Am7 G F#m G | C/E G/D Am7/C D | G

Bread of life

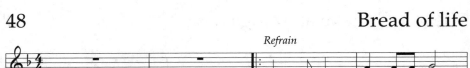

Bread of life, hope of the world,

Je-sus Christ, our broth-er:____ feed us now, give us life,

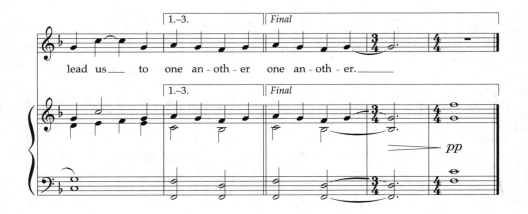

lead us___ to one an-oth-er one an-oth-er._____

Verses

1 As we pro-claim your death, as we re-call your life,
2 This bread we break and share was scat-tered once as grain:
3 We eat this liv-ing bread, we drink this sav-ing cup:

we re-mem-ber your prom - ise_____
just as now it is gath - ered,_____
sign of hope in our bro - ken world,___

to re-turn a - gain._____
make your peo - ple one._____
source of last - ing love._____

Additional alternate verses on the next page.

Alternate Verses

VERSES for Advent:

1   Be with your people, Lord, send us your saving Word:
    Jesus Christ, light of gladness, come among us now. *Refrain*

2   Bring to our world of fear the truth we long to hear:
    Jesus Christ, hope of ages, come to save us now. *Refrain*

VERSES for Christmas:

1   A child is born for us, a son is given to us,
    in our midst, Christ, our Lord and God comes as one who serves. *Refrain*

2   With our own eyes we see, with our own ears we hear
    the salvation of all the world, God's incarnate Word. *Refrain*

3   You are the hope of all, our promise and our call,
    radiant light in our darkness, truth to set us free. *Refrain*

VERSES for Lent:

1   Our hunger for your Word, our thirsting for your truth,
    are the sign of your life in us till we rest in you. *Refrain*

2   To those whose eyes are blind you give a light to see;
    dawn of hope in the midst of pain, love which sets us free. *Refrain*

Alternate Verses for Ordinary Time:

1   Hold us in unity, in love for all to see;
    that the world may believe in you, God of all who live. *Refrain*

2   You are the bread of peace, you are the wine of joy,
    broken now for your people, poured in endless love. *Refrain*

From hand to hand

From hand to hand, from hand to hand we
From hand to hand, from hand to hand we

pass the Bread of Life._____ From heart to heart, from
pass the cup of wine._____ From heart to heart, from

heart to heart, we pass the bread with love._____
heart to heart, we pass the cup with love._____

Optional Descant

Ha - le - lu - jah, thank you, Lord.

1 Let us tal - ents and tongues em - ploy, reach - ing out with a
2 Christ is a - ble to make us one, at his ta - ble he
3 Je - sus calls us in, sends us out bear - ing fruit in a

shout of joy: bread is bro - ken, wine is poured,
sets the tone, teach - ing peo - ple to live to bless,
world of doubt, gives us love to tell, bread to share:

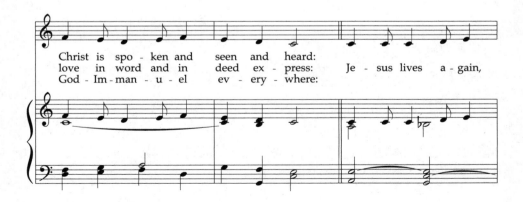

Christ is spo - ken and seen and heard: Je - sus lives a - gain,
love in word and in deed ex - press:
God - Im - man - u - el ev - ery - where:

earth can breathe a - gain, pass the word a - round: loaves a - bound.

Words: Fred Kaan (b. 1929).
Music: *Linstead*, Traditional Jamaican Melody, arr. Doreen Potter (1925-1980).
Words and Music © Oxford University Press/Church of Scotland, 198 Madison Ave., New York, NY 10016-4314 [www.oup.org].
All rights reserved. Used by permission.

Gentle Jesus, risen Lord

Verses
Cantor

All

1 Gen - tle Je - sus, ris - en Lord,
2 Bring-ing gifts of all we are,
3 In your bod - y we find life,
4 Je - sus Sav - ior, liv - ing bread!

we come to your

D   G   D

Cantor

ta - ble;

with our hearts so full of joy,
gifts of life and love and joy,
life you give for us to share,
bread of heav - en, bread of hope,

A   D   G   D

All

we come to your ta - ble.

A   D

Refrain

We come, we come, we come to your

ta - ble. We come, we come,

we come to your ta - ble.

All who hunger gather gladly

1 All who hun-ger gath-er glad-ly; ho-ly man-na
2 All who hun-ger, nev-er stran-gers, seek-er, be a
3 All who hun-ger, sing to-geth-er, Je-sus Christ is

is our bread. Come from wil-der-ness and wan-d'ring.
wel-come guest. Come from rest-less-ness and roam-ing.
liv-ing bread. Come from lone-li-ness and long-ing.

Here in truth we will be fed. You that yearn for
Here, in joy we keep the feast. We that once were
Here, in peace, we have been fed. Blest are those who

days of full-ness, all a-round us is our food.
lost and scat-tered in com-mun-ion's love have stood.
from this ta-ble live their days in grat-i-tude.

Taste and see the grace e-ter-nal.
Taste and see the grace e-ter-nal.
Taste and see the grace e-ter-nal.

Taste and see that God is good.
Taste and see that God is good.
Taste and see that God is good.

Words: Sylvia G. Dunstan (1955-1993) © GIA Publications, Inc., 7404 South Mason Ave., Chicago, IL 60638 [www.giamusic.com]. All rights reserved.
Used by permission.
Music: *Holy Manna*, from *The Southern Harmony*, 1835.
You must contact GIA Publications, Inc. to reproduce these words.

Let us now depart in your peace

53

Let us now de-part in your peace, bless-ed Je - sus.

Send us to our homes with God's love in our hearts.___

Let not the bus - y world claim all our loy - al - ties.

optional

Keep us ev - er mind - ful, dear Lord, of thee. A - men.

May the God of hope *Dios de la esperanza*

1 May the God of hope go with us ev - ery day,___
2 God will be our shep - herd as we go our way___

1 ¡Dios de la es - pe - ran - za, da - nos go - zo y paz!___
2 Dios se - rá nues - tro pas - tor en el ca - mi - no___

fill - ing all our lives with love and joy and peace.___
and will not for - sake us when we go a - stray.___

Al mun - do en cri - sis, ha - bla tu ver - dad.___
no nos a - ban - do - na - rá cuan - do nos per - di - mos.

May the God of jus - tice speed us on our way,___
E - ven though the load of life is hard to bear,___

Dios de la jus - ti - cia, mán - da - nos tu luz,___
La ___ vi - da es un - a car - ga pe - sa - da,___

bring-ing light and hope to ev - ery land and race.___
we must not for - get that God is al - ways there.___
luz y es - pe - ran - za en la os - cu - ri - dad.___
Pe - ro Dios siem - pre nos a - yu - da - rá.___

D7   G

Refrain

Pray - ing,___ let us work for peace; sing - ing,___ share our
O - re - mos___ por la paz,___ can - te - mos___

G   Am   D7

joy with all;___ work - ing___ for a world that's new,
de tu a - mor.___ Lu - che - mos por la paz,_

G   Am

faith - ful_____ when we hear Christ's call.___
fie - les_____ a_____ ti, Se - ñor.___

D7   G

May the Lord, mighty God

May the Lord,— might-y God, bless and

keep us for-ev - er; grant us peace,—

per-fect peace, cour-age in ev-ery en-deav - our.

Lift up and see his face, his

Lift up your eyes and see his face and his

grace for ev - er; may the Lord,

grace for ev - er; may the Lord,—

might-y God, bless and keep us for-ev - er.

might-y God, bless and keep us for-ev - er.

Words: Traditional Liturgical Text.
Music: *Wen Ti*, Chinese Origin, adapt. I-to Loh (b. 1936) © 1983 Abingdon Press (admin. T.C.C. - The Copyright Co., 1026 16th Ave. South, Nashville, TN 37212 [www.thecopyrightco.com]). All rights reserved. International copyright secured. Used by permission.
You must contact T.C.C. to reproduce this music.

May the Lord bless us and keep us,

and make his face to shine u-pon us

and be mer - ci - ful, mer - ci -

ful,   un -   -   to   us.

us.

May also be sung unaccompanied.

Words: Aaronic Blessing, adapt.
Music: Fiona Vidal-White © 2004 Fiona Vidal-White.
All rights reserved. Used by permission.

57 La paz del Señor *The peace of our God*

Em
1–3 La paz del Se - ñor, la paz del Se - ñor,
1–3 *The peace of the Lord, the peace of the Lord,*

Am **B7**

Em **C** **B7** **E7**
la paz del Re - su - ci - ta - do,____
the peace of the One who is ris - en,____

Am **D7** **G** **C**
la paz del Se - ñor a ti y a mi,
(2) se ha - ce pre - sen - te a hora ya quí,
(3) no pue - de vi - vir encer - ra̱da en si,
the peace of the Lord to you and me,
(2) *peace makes it - self pre - sent here and now.*
(3) *should not be en - closed in you or me,*

Am **B** **Em** (E7) *D.C. after each repeat*
a to - dos al can - za rá.____
a - pré - sta - te re - ci - bir - la.
a - pré - sta - te com - par - tir - la.
to ev - ery - one reach - es out.____
Be rea - dy God's peace to re - ceive.____
but shared a - mong all who be - lieve.____

Christ is coming

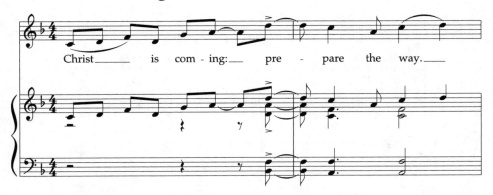

Christ is com - ing: pre - pare the way.

Christ is com - ing: pre - pare the way.

Fine

Christ is come - ing. Christ is come - ing.

D.C.

Words and Music: Edward V. Bonnemere, adapt. *Advent Jazz Vespers II* © Amity Music Corporation, 1475 Gaylord Terrace, Teaneck, NJ 07666.

59

Longing for light

Refrain

Christ, be our light! Shine in our hearts.

G   C   G   Em   Bm

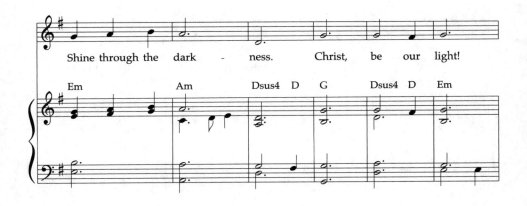

Shine through the dark - ness. Christ, be our light!

Em   Am   Dsus4   D   G   Dsus4   D   Em

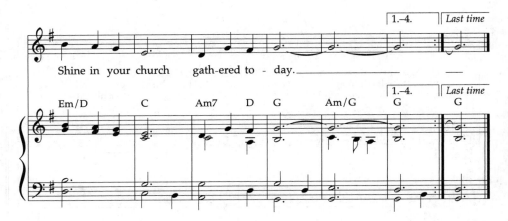

Shine in your church gath-ered to - day.

1.–4. | Last time

Em/D   C   Am7   D   G   Am/G   G   G

1.–4. | Last time

My heart sings out with joyful praise

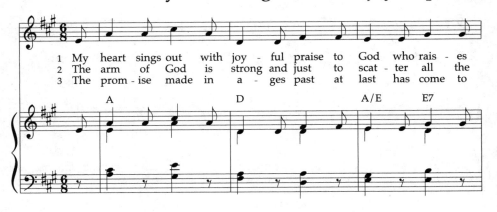

1 My heart sings out with joy - ful praise to God who rais - es
2 The arm of God is strong and just to scat - ter all the
3 The prom - ise made in a - ges past at last has come to

A   D   A/E   E7

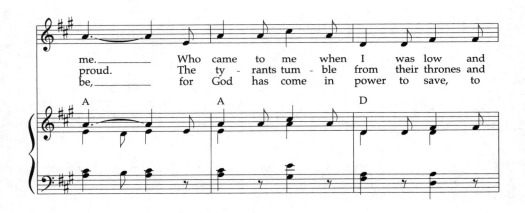

me._____ Who came to me when I was low and
proud. The ty - rants tum - ble from their thrones and
be,_____ for God has come in power to save, to

A   A   D

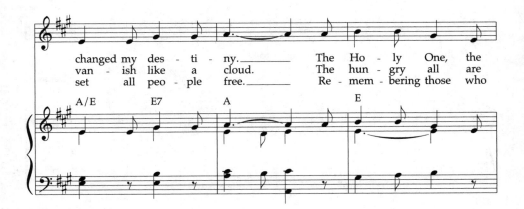

changed my des - ti - ny._____ The Ho - ly One, the
van - ish like a cloud. The hun - gry all are
set all peo - ple free._____ Re - mem - bering those who

A/E   E7   A   E

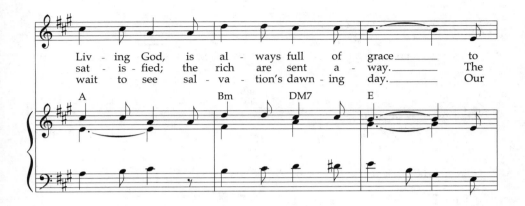

Liv - ing God, is al - ways full of grace_____ to
sat - is - fied; the rich are sent a - way._____ The
wait to see sal - va - tion's dawn - ing day._____ Our

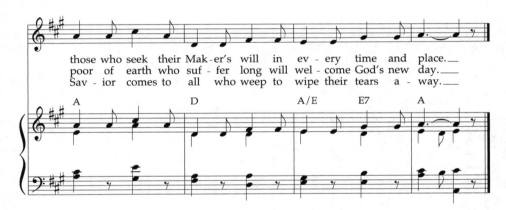

those who seek their Mak-er's will in ev - ery time and place._
poor of earth who suf - fer long will wel - come God's new day._
Sav - ior comes to all who weep to wipe their tears a - way._

Words: Ruth Duck.
Music: *Marias Lovsäng*, Swedish Folk Melody, arr. John L. Hooker (b. 1944) © GIA Publications, Inc. 7404 S. Mason Ave., Chicago, IL 60638
[www.giamusic.com]. Used by permission. All rights reserved.
You must contact GIA Publications, Inc. to reproduce this music.

Prepare the way of the Lord

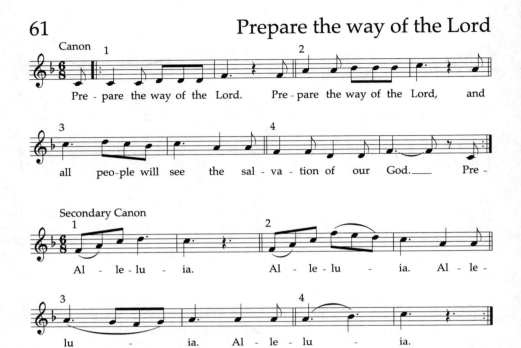

Canon

1 Pre - pare the way of the Lord. 2 Pre - pare the way of the Lord, and
3 all peo-ple will see the sal - va - tion of our God.___ Pre -

Secondary Canon

1 Al - le - lu - ia. 2 Al - le - lu - ia. Al - le -
3 lu - ia. Al - le - lu - ia.

Accompaniment

Capo I: (E) (A) (E)
F Bb F

Words: based on *Luke 3:4, 6*, adapt. The Taizé Community.
Music: Jacques Berthier (1923-1994) © 1984 by Les Presses de Taizé (France). (Words and Music admin. GIA Publications, Inc.,
7404 S. Mason Ave., Chicago, IL 60638 [www.giamusic.com].) All rights reserved. Used by permission.
You must contact GIA Publications, Inc. to reproduce this selection.

Stay awake, be ready

Words and Music: Christopher Walker (b. 1947) © 1988, 1989, 1990 OCP Publications, 5536 NE Hassalo, Portland, OR 97213 [www.ocp.org].
All rights reserved. Used by permission.
You must contact OCP Publications to reproduce this selection.

Prepare ye the way

Pre-pare ye the way___ of the Lord.___

Pre-pare ye the way___ of the Lord.___

1.–4. |Final   Fine

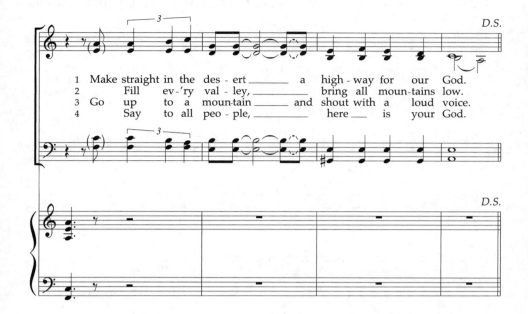

1 Make straight in the des - ert _____ a high - way for our God.
2 Fill ev-'ry val - ley, _____ bring all moun-tains low.
3 Go up to a moun-tain _____ and shout with a loud voice.
4 Say to all peo - ple, _____ here __ is your God.

Words: *Isaiah 40:3-4, 9.*
Music: James E. Moore, Jr. (b. 1951) © 1992 GIA Publications, Inc., 7404 South Mason Ave., Chicago, IL 60638 [www.giamusic.com].

Gloria, gloria, gloria   64

¡Glo - ria, glo - ria, glo - ria__ en las al - tu - ras a Dios!
Glo - ry, glo - ry, glo - ry,__ glo - ry to God on high

y en la tie - rra paz pa-ra a-qué-llos que a-ma el Se - ñor.__
and on earth peace to all peo - ple in whom God is well pleased.

Words: Traditional.
Music: Pablo Sosa (b. 1933) © Pablo Sosa.

Jesus our brother, kind and good

1 Je - sus our broth - er, kind and good, was hum - bly
2 "I," said the don - key, shag - gy and brown, "I car - ried his
3 "I," said the cow, all white and red, "I gave him my

Capo 5: (C) (G7) (C)
F C7 F

born in a sta - ble rude, and the friend - ly beasts a -
moth-er up - hill and down. I car - ried his moth-er to
man - ger for his bed. I gave him my hay to

(F) (G7) (C) (F)
Bb C7 F Bb

round him stood, Je - sus our broth - er, kind and good.
Beth-le - hem town. I," said the don - key shag-gy and brown.
pil - low his head. I," said the cow all white and red.

(Dm) (Em) (C) (G7) (C)
Gm Am F C7 F

4 "I," said the sheep with curly horn,
   "I gave him my wool for his blanket warm.
   He wore my coat on Christmas morn.
   I," said the sheep with curly horn.

5 "I," said the dove from rafters high,
   "I cooed him to sleep, so he should not cry.
   We cooed him to sleep, my mate and I.
   I," said the dove from rafters high.

6 Thus every beast by some good spell,
   in the stable dark was glad to tell
   of the gift he gave Emmanuel,
   the gift he gave Emmanuel.

Words: att. Robert Davis (1881-1950).
Music: Pierre de Corbiel, arr. Margaret W. Mealy (b. 1922) © 1961 General Convention of the Episcopal Church. All rights reserved. Used by permission.

Sleep, sleep, gently sleep

66

Words and Music: *Sleep, Sleep, Gently Sleep*, Judith Franklin, arr. June Baker (b. 1936) © 1995 Stainer & Bell Ltd. and Methodist Church (UK)
Division of Education and Youth (admin. Hope Publishing Co., 380 S. Main Pl., Carol Stream, IL 60188 [www.hopepublishing.com]). All rights reserved.
Used by permission.
You must contact Hope Publishing to reproduce this selection.

The Virgin Mary had a baby boy

1 The Vir - gin Mar - y had a ba - by boy, __ the
2 The an - gels sang when the ba - by born, __ the
3 The wise men saw where the ba - by born, __ the

Capo 3: (D)   (A7)
F   C7

Vir - gin Mar - y had a ba - by boy, __ the
an - gels sang when the ba - by born, __ the
wise men saw where the ba - by born, __ the

(D)
F

Vir - gin Mar - y had a ba - by boy, __ and they
an - gels sang____ when the ba - by born, __ and they
wise men went____ where the ba - by born, __ and they

(D7)   (G)   (Em)
F7   Bb   Gm

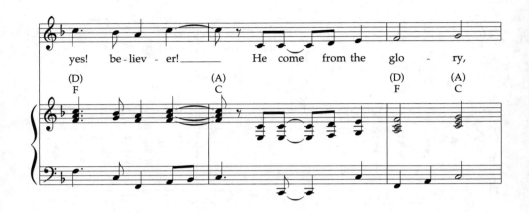

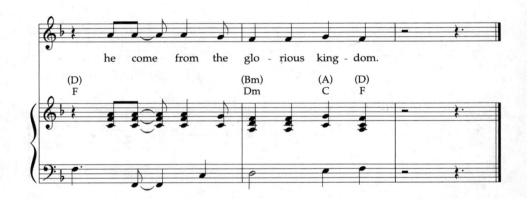

Listen, my friends

68

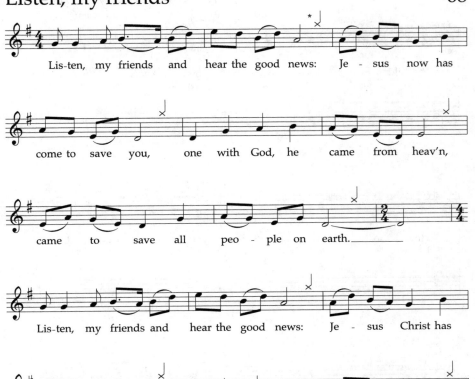

Lis-ten, my friends and hear the good news: Je - sus now has

come to save you, one with God, he came from heav'n,

came to save all peo - ple on earth.___

Lis-ten, my friends and hear the good news: Je - sus Christ has

come to bring hope, one with God, he came to save me;

came to save me, came to save you!___

* *finger cymbals*

Words: Anon. Chinese, tr. Lucy Ding, para. C. Michael Hawn © 1999 Choristers Guild, 2834 West Kingsley Road, Garland, TX 75041-2498 [www.choristersguild.org]. All rights reserved. Used by permission.
Music: Traditional Chinese.

Child so lovely *Niño lindo*

Child so love-ly, here I kneel be-fore you,
Ni - ño lin - do, an - te ti me rin - do,

child so love-ly, you are Christ, my God.
ni - ño lin - do, e - res tú mi Dios.

Child so love-ly, here I kneel be-fore you,
Ni - ño lin - do, an - te ti me rin - do;

child so love-ly, you are Christ, the Lord.
ni - ño lin - do, e - res tú mi Dios.

That boy-child of Ma - ry was born in a sta - ble, a man-ger his cra - dle in Beth - le - hem.

Fine

1 What shall we
2 His name is
3 How can he
4 Gift of the
5 One with the
6 Glad - ly we

call him,	child of the man - ger?	What name is
Je - sus,	God ev - er with us,	God giv - en
save us,	how can he help us,	born here a -
Fa - ther,	to hu - man moth - er,	makes him our
Fa - ther,	he is our Sav - ior,	heav - en - sent
praise him,	love and a - dore him,	give our - selves

D.C.

giv - en	in Beth - le - hem?
for us	in Beth - le - hem?
mong us	in Beth - le - hem?
broth - er	in Beth - le - hem?
help - er	in Beth - le - hem?
to him	in Beth - le - hem?

Words: based on *Luke 2:7*, adapt. Tom Colvin (b. 1925).
Music: *Blantyre*, Traditional Malawi melody, adapt. Tom Colvin (b. 1925).

Los magos que llegaron a Belén
The magi who to Bethlehem did go

Los ma-gos que lle-ga-ron a Be-lén a-nun-
The ma-gi who to Beth-le-hem did go were the

cia-ron la lle-ga-da del Me-sí-as y no-so-tros, con a-le-
her-alds of the com-ing of Mes-si-ah; and with joy we al-so would

grí-a, la a-nun-cia-mos hoy tam-bién.
has-ten to an-nounce the news to-day.

Verses

1 De tie-rra le-ja-na ve-ni-mos a ver-te,
2 Al re-cién na-ci-do que es Rey de los re-yes,

1 *From a dis-tant land we come with hum-ble greet-ing,*
2 *To the new-born Child who has no earth-ly trea-sure*

nos sir-ve de guí-a la es-tre-lla de O-rien-te. __
o-ro le re-ga-lo pa-ra or-nar sus sie-nes. __

where the east-ern star our car-a-van is lead-ing. __
I have come with gold to bring de-light and plea-sure. __

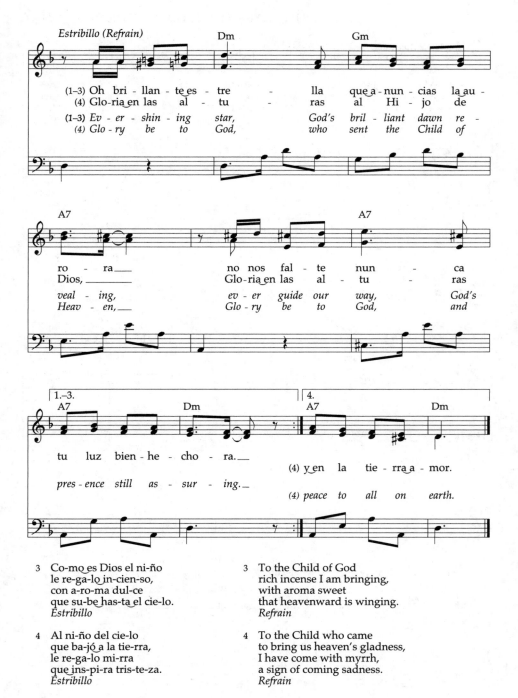

Estribillo (Refrain)

(1–3) Oh bri - llan - te es - tre - - lla que a - nun - cias la au -
(4) Glo - ria en las al - tu - - ras al Hi - jo de

(1–3) *Ev - er - shin - ing star,* *God's bril - liant dawn re -*
(4) *Glo - ry be to God,* *who sent the Child of*

ro - ra____ no nos fal - te nun - - ca
Dios,____ Glo - ria en las al - tu - - ras

veal - ing, *ev - er guide our way,* *God's*
Heav - en,____ *Glo - ry be to God,* *and*

1.–3.
tu luz bien - he - cho - ra.____

pres - ence still as - sur - ing.____

4.
(4) y en la tie - rra a - mor.

(4) *peace to all on earth.*

3 Co - mo es Dios el ni - ño
le re - ga - lo in - cien - so,
con a - ro - ma dul - ce
que su - be has - ta el cie - lo.
Estribillo

3 To the Child of God
rich incense I am bringing,
with aroma sweet
that heavenward is winging.
Refrain

4 Al ni - ño del cie - lo
que ba - jó a la tie - rra,
le re - ga - lo mi - rra
que ins - pi - ra tris - te - za.
Estribillo

4 To the Child who came
to bring us heaven's gladness,
I have come with myrrh,
a sign of coming sadness.
Refrain

Words: Manuel Fernández Juncas, tr. Carolyn Jennings © 1995 The Pilgrim Press, 700 Prospect Ave., Cleveland, OH 44115-1100
[www.thepilgrimpress.com]. All rights reserved. Used by permission.
Music: *Los Magos*, Traditional Puerto Rican Carol

Who are these eastern strangers?

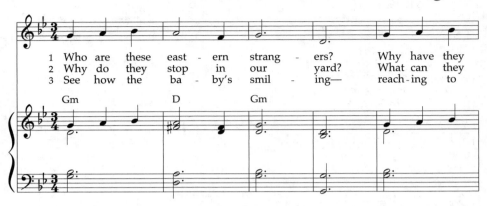

1 Who are these east - ern strang - ers? Why have they
2 Why do they stop in our yard? What can they
3 See how the ba - by's smil - ing— reach-ing to

come so far?_____ Why do they gaze in -
hope to see?_____ Why do they come with
hold the myrrh!_____ Why is his mo - ther

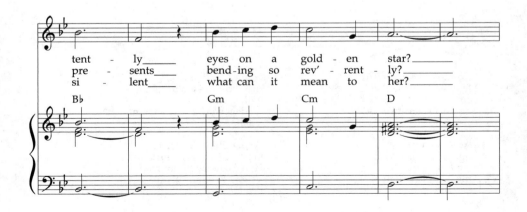

tent - ly_____ eyes on a gold - en star?_____
pre - sents_____ bend -ing so rev' - rent - ly?_____
si - lent_____ what can it mean to her?_____

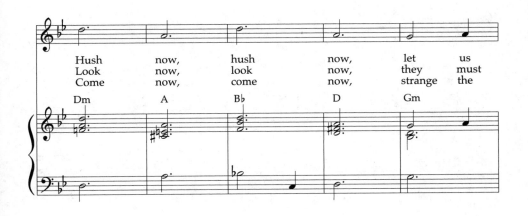

Hush now, hush now, let us
Look now, look now, they must
Come now, come now, let strange the

Dm   A   Bb   D   Gm

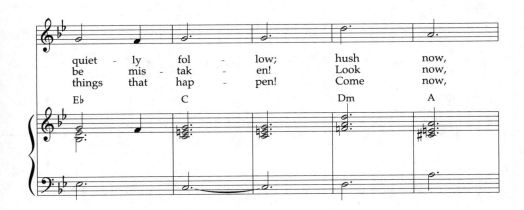

quiet - ly fol - low; hush now,
be mis - tak - en! Look now,
things that hap - pen! Come now,

Eb   C   Dm   A

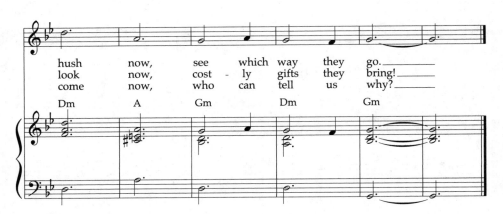

hush now, see which way they go._____
look now, cost - ly gifts they bring!
come now, who can tell us why?_____

Dm   A   Gm   Dm   Gm

Words: Cecily Taylor.
Music: *Eastern Strangers*, Mike Daymond.
Words and Music © 1999 Stainer & Bell Ltd. (admin. Hope Publishing Co., 380 S. Main Pl., Carol Stream, IL 60188 [www.hopepublishing.com].)

73

Look up!

1 Look up! Look up! Look up! See the light of the
pro - phets.* Look up! Look up! Look up! See the
light of the pro - phets.* For the word of the Lord is a
light, shin - ing in the dark - ness___ un - til the
day dawns, and the Morn - ing Star a - ris - es in your hearts.

*2 angels, 3 star, 4 Jesus

Words: based on *2 Peter 1:19*.
Music: June Fischer Armstrong © 1991 CRC Publications, 2850 Kalamazoo Avenue Southeast, Grand Rapids, MI 49560
[www.crcpublications.org]. All rights reserved. Used by permission.

Blest are the poor in spirit

Antiphon *(also hummed during Cantor verses)*

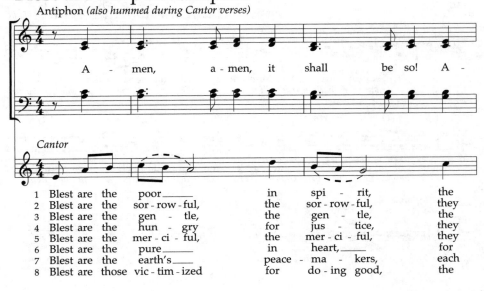

A - men, a - men, it shall be so! A -

Cantor

1	Blest are the	poor___		in	spi - rit,	the
2	Blest are the	sor - row - ful,		the	sor - row - ful,	they
3	Blest are the	gen - tle,		the	gen - tle,	the
4	Blest are the	hun - gry		for	jus - tice,	they
5	Blest are the	mer - ci - ful,		the	mer - ci - ful,	they
6	Blest are the	pure___		in	heart,___	for
7	Blest are the	earth's___		peace - ma - kers,		each
8	Blest are those vic - tim - ized			for	do - ing good,	the

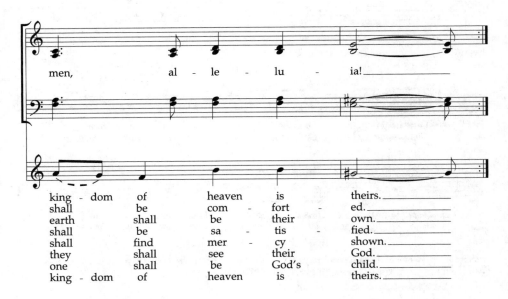

men,	al - le - lu - ia!___
king - dom	of	heaven	is	theirs.___
shall	be	com - fort - ed.___
earth	shall	be	their	own.___
shall	be	sa - tis - fied.___
shall	find	mer - cy	shown.___
they	shall	see	their	God.___
one	shall	be	God's	child.___
king - dom	of	heaven	is	theirs.___

Yo soy la luz del mundo
I am the world's true light

Part 1

Yo soy la luz del mun - do. El que me si - ga ten - drá ta
I am the world's true light. If you will fol - low me, your

luz que le da la vi - da. Y nun - ca an - da - rá en la os - cu - ri - dad.
life will re-flect my bright - ness and you'll nev - er walk in the night.

Part 2

A - le - lu - ya, a - le - lu - ya,

a - le - lu - ya, a - le - lu! La, la, la, la, la, la.

Part 3

Dios es la luz, Dios es la paz, Dios es a - mor.
God is our light, God is our peace, God is our love.

Dios es la luz, Dios es la paz, Dios es a - mor.
God is our light, God is our peace, God is our love.

Words and Music: based on *John 8:1*, att. Rudolfo Ascencio, tr. C. Michael Hawn © 1999 Choristers Guild, 2834 West Kingsley Road, Garland, TX 75041-2498 [www.choristersguild.org]. All rights reserved. Used by permission.

When Jesus saw the fishermen
76

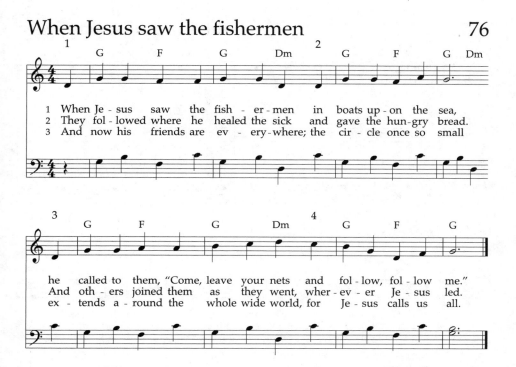

1 When Je - sus saw the fish - er - men in boats up - on the sea,
2 They fol - lowed where he healed the sick and gave the hun-gry bread.
3 And now his friends are ev - ery-where; the cir - cle once so small

he called to them, "Come, leave your nets and fol - low, fol - low me."
And oth - ers joined them as they went, wher - ev - er Je - sus led.
ex - tends a - round the whole wide world, for Je - sus calls us all.

Words: Edith Agnew © 1963 W.L. Jenkins, from *Songs and Hymns for Primary Children* [admin. Westminster John Knox Press, 100 Witherspoon St., Louisville, KY 40202-1396 [www.ppcbooks.com].] All rights reserved. Used by permission.
Music: *St. Stephen*, Richard L. Van Oss © 1994 CRC Publications, 2850 Kalamazoo Avenue Southeast, Grand Rapids, MI 49560 [www.crcpublications.org]. All rights reserved. Used by permission.

I, the Lord of sea and sky

1 I, the Lord of sea and sky, I have heard my
2 I, the Lord of snow and rain, I have borne my
3 I, the Lord of wind and flame, I will tend the

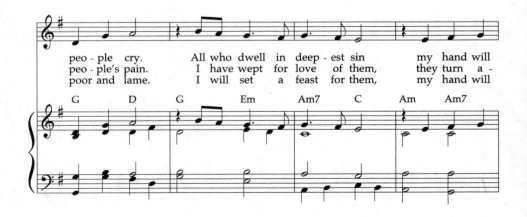

peo - ple cry. All who dwell in deep - est sin my hand will
peo - ple's pain. I have wept for love of them, they turn a -
poor and lame. I will set a feast for them, my hand will

save.   I who made the stars of night,
way.   I will break their hearts of stone,
save.   Fin-est bread I will pro - vide

D   G   D   G   C/G   G

I   will make   their dark - ness bright.   Who will bear   my
give them hearts for love a - lone.   I   will speak   my
till their hearts be sat - is - fied.   I   will give   my

        C/G   G   D   G   Em

light   to them?   Whom shall I   send?_____
word to them.   Whom shall I   send?_____
life   to them.   Whom shall I   send?_____

Am7   C   Am   Am7   D

Here I am, Lord.____ Is it I, Lord?____ I have heard you call-ing in the night._____ I will go, Lord,____ if you lead me,____ I will hold your peo - ple in my

1. 2.
heart._____

3.
heart._____

We will lay our burden down

78

1. We will lay _____ our bur-den down, we will lay _____ our bur-den down, we will lay _____ our bur-den down in the hands of the ris-en Lord. _____
2. We will light _____ the flame of love, we will light _____ the flame of love, we will light _____ the flame of love as the hands of the ris-en Lord. _____
3. We will show _____ both hurt and hope, we will show _____ both hurt and hope, we will show _____ both hurt and hope like the hands of the ris-en Lord. _____
4. We will walk _____ the path of peace, we will walk _____ the path of peace, we will walk _____ the path of peace hand in hand with the ris-en Lord. _____

* The accompaniment may be sung by a choir using the words above.

Sent by the Lord

Sent by the Lord am I; my hands are rea - dy now to

make the earth the place in which the king - dom comes. Sent

by the Lord am I; my hands are rea - dy now to

make the earth the place in which the king - dom comes. The

an - gels can - not change a world of hurt and pain in -

Ah

an - gels can - not change a world of hurt and pain in -

Ah

80

The light of Christ

The light of Christ has come in - to the

The light of Christ has come in -

C   F   Dm

world. The light of Christ has

to the world. The light of Christ

G   C

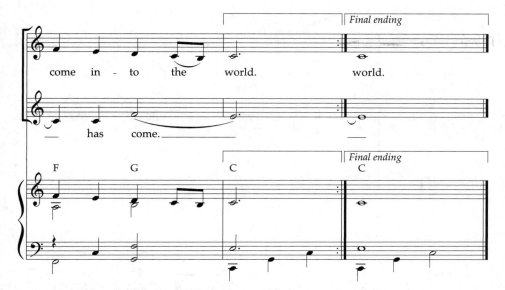

Your word

Your word, *(your word,)* your word *(your word,)* is a

lamp to my feet. Your word, *(your word,)* your

word *(your word)* is a lamp to my feet, and a

light to my path. *(and a light to my*

(G) (A7) (D) (G)
Ab Bb7 Eb Ab

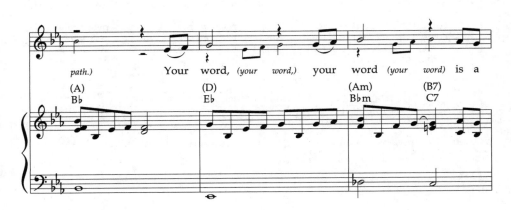

path.) Your word, *(your word,)* your word *(your word)* is a

(A) (D) (Am) (B7)
Bb Eb Bbm C7

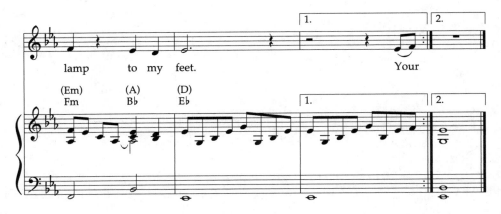

lamp to my feet. Your

(Em) (A) (D)
Fm Bb Eb

1. 2.

Words: *Psalm 119:105.*
Music: Frank Hernandez © 1990, Birdwing Music (ASCAP) (admin. EMI Christian Music Publishing, PO Box 5085, Brentwood, TN 37024-5085).
All rights reserved. Used by permission.

Come now, O Prince of Peace

1 Come now O Prince of Peace, make us one bo - dy,
2 Come now, O God of love, make us one bo - dy,
3 Come now and set us free, O God, our Sa - viour,
4 Come, Hope of u - ni - ty, make us one bo - dy,

come, O Lord Je - sus, re - con - cile your peo - ple.
come, O Lord Je - sus, re - con - cile your peo - ple.
come, O Lord Je - sus, re - con - cile all na - tions.
come, O Lord Je - sus, re - con - cile all na - tions.

If you love me

1 If you love me, tru-ly love me, keep my com-mand-ments
2 If you love me, tru-ly love me, come now and my dis-
4 If you love me, tru-ly love me, in-to the world a-

day by day. If you love me, tru-ly love me,
ci - ple be. If you love me, tru-ly love me,
rise and go. If you love me, tru-ly love me,

Fine

fol - low for-ev - er in my way.
fol - low and so re - mem - ber me. *to verse three*
there ev - 'ry-where my wit - ness show.

3 Through the land my peo - ple feed, al - le - lu - ia,

in their sor - row, in their need, al - le - lu - ia.

Forty days and forty nights

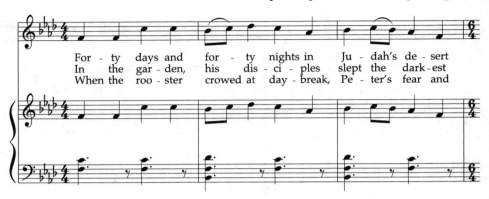

For - ty days and for - ty nights in Ju - dah's de - sert
In the gar - den, his dis - ci - ples slept the dark - est
When the roo - ster crowed at day - break, Pe - ter's fear and

Je - sus stayed. All a - lone he fought temp - ta - tion,
hours a - way. but our Lord did not con - demn them
pan - ic grew. He de - nied three times the charge that

all a - lone he fast - ed, prayed. When the heat of
when they would not watch or pray. Make me con - stant
Je - sus was a man he knew. When my love for

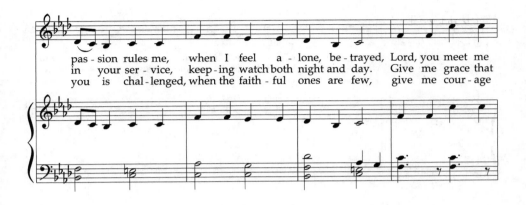

pas - sion rules me, when I feel a - lone, be - trayed, Lord, you meet me
in your ser - vice, keep-ing watch both night and day. Give me grace that
you is chal - lenged, when the faith - ful ones are few, give me cour - age

in the de-sert, strong in faith and un - a-fraid.
I may ne - ver such a love as yours be-tray.
and con - vic-tion to pro-claim my Lord a - new.

God it was

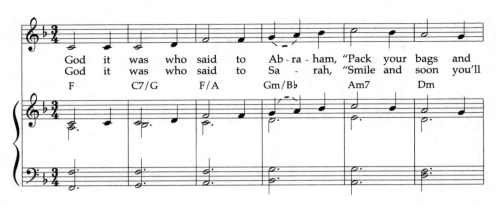

God it was who said to Ab-ra-ham, "Pack your bags and
God it was who said to Sa - rah, "Smile and soon you'll

F   C7/G   F/A   Gm/Bb   Am7   Dm

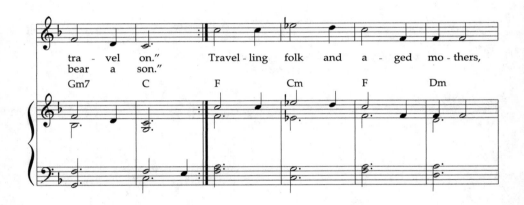

tra - vel on."   Travel-ling folk and a - ged mo-thers,
bear a son."

Gm7   C   F   Cm   F   Dm

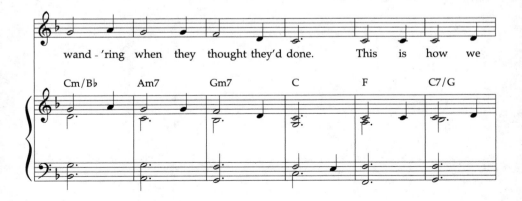

wand -'ring when they thought they'd done.   This is how we

Cm/Bb   Am7   Gm7   C   F   C7/G

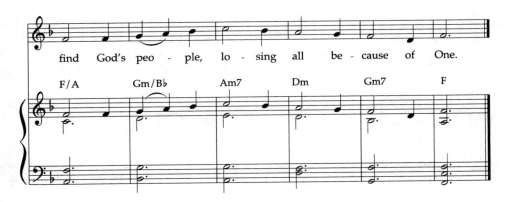

find God's peo - ple, lo - sing all be - cause of One.

F/A   Gm/B♭   Am7   Dm   Gm7   F

Choose verse according to lectionary, ending with stanza five.

2   God it was who said to Moses,
    "Save my people, part the sea."
    God it was who said to Miriam,
    "Sing and dance to show you're free."
    Shepherd-saints and tambourinists
    doing what God knew they could—
    this is how we find God's people,
    liberating what they should.

3   God it was who said to Joseph,
    "Down your tools and take your wife."
    God it was who said to Mary,
    "In your womb, I'll start my life!"
    Carpenter and country maiden
    leaving town and trade and skills—
    this is how we find God's people,
    moved by what their Maker wills.

4   Christ it was who said, "Zacchaeus,
    I would like to eat with you."
    Christ it was who said to Martha,
    "Listening's what you need to do."
    Civil servants and housekeepers,
    changing places at a cost—
    this is how Christ summons people,
    calling both the loved and lost.

5   In this crowd which spans the ages,
    with these saints whom we revere,
    God wants us to share their purpose
    starting now and starting here.
    So we celebrate our calling,
    so we raise both heart and voice,
    as we pray that through our living
    more may find they are God's choice.

Words: John L. Bell (b. 1949) and Graham Maule.
Music: Traditional Scots Gaelic, arr. John L. Bell (b. 1949) and Graham Maule.
Words and Music © 1989, 2002 WGRG The Iona Community (Scotland) (admin. GIA Publications, Inc.,
7404 South Mason Ave., Chicago, IL 60638 [www.giamusic.com].) All rights reserved. Used by permission.
You must contact GIA Publications, Inc. to reproduce this selection.

In the bulb there is a flower

1 In the bulb there is a flow - er; in the seed, an ap - ple
2 There's a song in ev - 'ry si - lence, seek-ing word and mel - o -
3 In our end is our be - gin - ning; in our time, in - fin - i -

tree; in co - coons, a hid - den prom - ise: but - ter -
dy; there's a dawn in ev - 'ry dark - ness, bring-ing
ty; in our doubt there is be - liev - ing; in our

flies will soon be free! In the cold and snow of
hope to you and me. From the past will come the
life, e - ter - ni - ty; in our death, a res - ur -

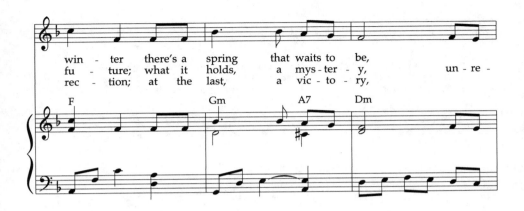

win - ter there's a spring that waits to be,
fu - ture; what it holds, a mys - ter - y,
rec - tion; at the last, a vic - to - ry,
un - re -

vealed un - til its sea - son, some-thing God a - lone can see.

I want Jesus to walk with me

1 I want Je - sus____ to walk with me (walk with me); I want
2 In my tri - als,____ Lord, walk with me (walk with me); In my
3 In my sor - rows,____ Lord, walk with me (walk with me); In my

Je - sus____ to walk with me (walk with me); All a -
tri - als,____ Lord, walk with me (walk with me); When the
sor - rows,____ Lord, walk with me (walk with me); When my

long my____ pil - grim jour - ney,____ Lord, I want
shades of____ life are fall - ing,____ Lord, I want
heart with - in____ is ach - ing,____ Lord, I want

Je - sus____ to walk with me (walk with me).
Je - sus____ to walk with me (walk with me).
Je - sus____ to walk with me (walk with me).

Jesus said, I am the door

1 Je - sus said, I am the door, knock and it shall be
2 Je - sus said, I am the way, mark my foot - steps
3 Je - sus said, I am the truth, seek life's trea - sure,
4 Je - sus said, I am the vine, you the branch - es,
5 Je - sus said, I am the light, bright - ly shin - ing,

op - ened un - to you. En - ter in, joy - ful - ly. Je - sus said,
mark my foot - steps, fol - low me, fol - low me. Je - sus said,
seek life's trea - sure, fol - low me, fol - low me. Je - sus said,
you the branch-es, part of me, part of me. Je - sus said,
bright-ly shin - ing, come to me, come to me. Je - sus said,

I am the door, en - ter, en - ter, joy - ful - ly.
I am the way, fol - low, fol - low, joy - ful - ly.
I am the truth, fol - low, fol - low, joy - ful - ly.
I am the vine, you the branch-es, part of me.
I am the light, shin - ing, shin - ing, come to me.

Words and Music: *Jesus Said*, Marlene Phillips © 1999 Stainer & Bell Ltd. (admin. Hope Publishing Co., 380 S. Main Pl., Carol Stream, IL 60188 [www. hopepublishing.com]). All rights reserved. Used by permission.
You must contact Hope Publishing to reproduce this selection.

89 What does it mean to follow Jesus?

Refrain

Capo 3: (G) Bb (C) Eb (D) F (G) Bb

What does it mean to fol - low Je - sus? What does it mean to

(D) F (G) Bb (C) Eb (G) Bb

go his way? What does it mean to do what he wants me to,

To verses (Am7) Cm7 (D) F *Last time* (Am7) Cm7 (D) F (G) Bb

ev - 'ry day? ev - 'ry day?

(C) Eb (D7) F7 (G) Bb (Am7) Cm7 (D) F (G) Bb

1 I can love my neigh-bor, just as Je - sus said.
2 I can say I'm sor - ry when I've done some wrong.

90

The King of glory comes

Refrain

The King of glo-ry comes, the na-tion re-joic-es.

O-pen the gates be-fore him, lift up your voic-es.

1 Who is the King of glo-ry? What shall we call him?
2 In all of Gal-i-lee, in cit-y or vil-lage,
3 He gave his life for us, the pledge of sal-va-tion;
4 He con-quered sin and death; he tru-ly has ris-en.

He is Im-man-u-el, the prom-ised of a-ges.
he goes a-mong his peo-ple, cur-ing their ill-ness.
he took up-on him-self the sin of the na-tions.
And he will share with us his heav-en-ly king-dom.

Repeat refrain

* Sing small notes as a descant on the final refrain.

Words: Willard F. Jabusch (b. 1930) © 1969, 1982 OCP Publications, 5536 NE Hassalo, Portland OR 97213 [www.ocp.org]. All rights reserved.
Used with permission.
Music: *Promised One,* arr. John Ferguson © 1974 United Church Press, Cleveland, OH [www.unitedchurchpress.com]. All rights reserved.
Used by permission.
You must contact OCP Publications to reproduce these words.

'Sanna

'San-na,* san-na-ni-na, san-na, san-na, san-na, _____ san - na, san - na, san - na, san-na-ni-na, san - na, san - na san - na. _____ San - _____

*This is a shortened form of the word 'hosanna.'

92

A new commandment

this shall all know you are my dis - ci - ples: if

you have love one for an - o - ther._____

Pan de Vida

Refrain

*Pan de Vi - da,_____ cuer - po del Se - ñor,_____

Capo 2: (G7sus4)   (C)   (F)   (G)
      A7sus4   D   G   A

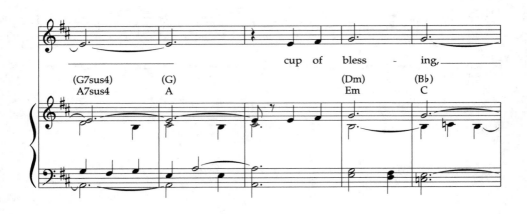

_____ cup of bless - ing,_____

(G7sus4)   (G)   (Dm)   (B♭)
A7sus4   A   Em   C

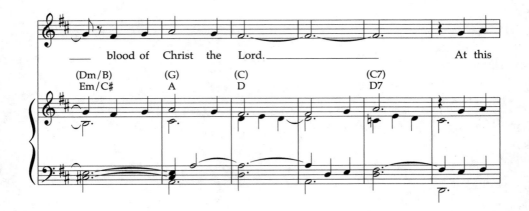

___ blood of Christ the Lord._____ At this

(Dm/B)   (G)   (C)   (C7)
Em/C#   A   D   D7

ta - ble_____ the last shall be first,_____

(F) (F/E) (Dm) (E7) (Am) (Am7/G)
G G/F# Em F#7 Bm Bm7/A

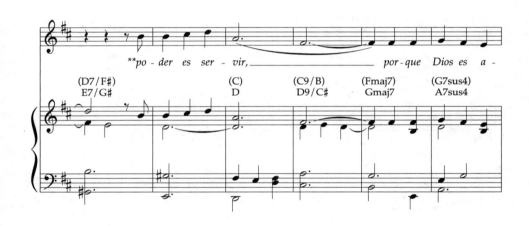

**po - der es ser - vir,_____ por - que Dios es a-

(D7/F#) (C) (C9/B) (Fmaj7) (G7sus4)
E7/G# D D9/C# Gmaj7 A7sus4

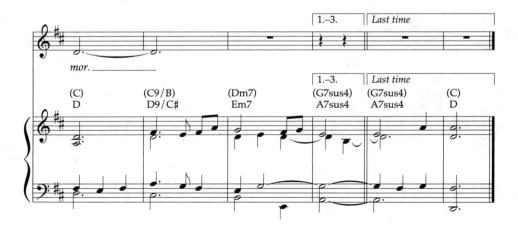

1.–3. | Last time

mor._____

1.–3. | Last time

(C) (C9/B) (Dm7) (G7sus4) (G7sus4) (C)
D D9/C# Em7 A7sus4 A7sus4 D

Verses

1 ⁂ We are the dwell-ing of God,_____
***2 Us - te - des me lla - man "Se - ñor,"_____ me in -
3 ⁂ There is no Jew ___ or Greek,_____

(F) (Bb/F) (F) (Bb/F)
G C/G G C/G

fra - gile and wound-ed and weak._____ We are the
cli - no a la - var - les los pies:_____ Ha - gan lo
there is no slave ___ or free:_____ there is no

(F) (G7/F) (C) (C9/Bb) (Am)
G A7/G D D9/C Bm

bod - y of Christ,_____ called to be_____ the com -
mis - mo, hu - mil - des, sir - vién - do - se
wom-an or man;_____ on - ly heirs_____ of the

(Am7/G) (Dsus4) (D7) (Dm) (Em)
Bm7/A Esus4 E7 Em F#m

D.C.

pas - sion	of	God.			
u - nos	a	o	-	-	-	tros.
prom-ise	of	God.			

(F) (G) (G7sus4) (G) (G7)
G   A   A7sus4   A   A7 D.C.

* Bread of Life, body of the Lord,
** power is for service because God is love.
*** You are the Lord, and I bow to wash your feet: you must do the same, humbly serving each other.

Words and Music: *John 13:1-15, Galatians 3:28-29,* Bob Hurd (b. 1950) and Pia Moriarty © 1988 OCP Publications, 5336 NE Hassalo,
Portland OR 92713 [www.ocp.org]. All rights reserved. Used by permission.
You must contact OCP Publications to reproduce this selection.

94 Brother, sister, let me serve you

1 Bro - ther, sis - ter, let me serve you, let me be as
2 We are pil - grims on a jour - ney, fel - low trav'l - lers
3 I will hold the Christ-light for you in the night - time
4 I will weep when you are weep - ing; when you laugh, I'll
5 When we sing to God in hea - ven, we shall find such
6 Bro - ther, sis - ter, let me serve you, let me be as

Christ to you; pray that I may have the grace to
on the road; we are here to help each o - ther
of your fear; I will hold my hand out to you,
laugh with you. I will share your joy and sor - row
har - mo - ny, born of all we've known to - geth - er
Christ to you; pray that I may have the grace to

let you be my ser - vant too.
walk the mile and bear the load.
speak the peace you long to hear.
till we've seen this jour - ney through.
of Christ's love and a - gon - y.
let you be my ser - vant, too.

Crashing waters at creation

1 Crash - ing wa - ters ___ at cre - a - tion
2 Part - ing wa - ter ___ stood and trem - bled
3 Cleans - ing wa - ter ___ once at Jor - dan
4 Liv - ing wa - ter, ___ nev - er end - ing,

or - dered by the Spi - rit's breath, first to wit - ness
as the cap - tives passed on through, wash - ing off ___ the
closed a - round the One fore - told, o - pened to ___ re -
quench the thirst and flood the soul. Well - spring, Source of

day's be - gin - ning from the bright - ness of night's death.
chains of bond - age— chan - nel to a life made new.
veal the glo - ry ev - er new and ev - er old.
life e - ter - nal, drench our dry - ness, make us whole.

Words: Sylvia G. Dunstan (1955-1993) © GIA Publications, Inc., 7404 South Mason Ave., Chicago, IL 60638 [www.giamusic.com]. All rights reserved.
Used by permission.
Music: *Restoration*, melody from *The Southern Harmony*, 1835.
You must contact GIA Publications, Inc. to reproduce these words.

walk a-long be-side___ us, our God will lead and
shore or in a des-ert land? So ma-ny shall your
now I laugh and sing for joy, so dance with me and

B7   Em   Am

guide___ us as we go to the prom-ised land."
chil-dren be—so ma-ny you can-not count."
sing with me; sing a new song of praise and joy.

Em   B7   Em

Reader:
The Lord said to Abraham,
"Leave your country, your people,
and your father's household.
Go to the land I will show you.
I will make you into a great nation,
and I will bless you." *Sing stanza 1*

The Lord took Abraham outside and said,
"Look up at the heavens and count the stars—
if indeed you can count them."
Then he said to him,
"So shall your children be." *Sing stanza 2*

The Lord said to Abraham,
"Your wife Sarah will bear you a son,
and you will call him Isaac.
I will establish my covenant with him
as an everlasting covenant."
The Lord did for Sarah what he had promised.
Sarah became pregnant
and bore a son to Abraham in his old age,
at the very time God had promised him. *Sing stanza 3*

Words: based on *Genesis 12:1-2, 15:5, 17:19, 21:1-2*, adapted Helen Walter.
Music: Emily R. Brink. Words and Music © 1993 CRC Publications, 2850 Kalamazoo Avenue Southeast, Grand Rapids, MI 49560
[www.crcpublications.org]. All rights reserved. Used by permission.

It rained on the earth forty days

1 It rained on the earth for-ty days, for-ty nights, and
2 God told A-bra-ham, "I will give you a land, a
3 When Je-sus the Christ came to live on the earth, God's
4 To us and our chil-dren the pro-mise is made if

all of the world was de-stroyed. The ark No-ah built at the
peo-ple as man-y as the stars." Though child-less and old, he and
pro-mise to us was ful-filled. His life and his death were a
we will but trust in his word. In bap-tism join-ing the

call-ing of God saved God's cho-sen ones from the flood. God
Sar-ah be-lieved and trust-ed the word of the Lord. God
new cov-e-nant, as-sur-ance of love full and free. God
peo-ple of God, we live in the power of his grace. God

gave to No-ah the rain-bow sign: "Such a flood I will not send a-
gave them I-saac, a son, at last, and this is the cov-enant he
gave his Son, his on-ly Son; to all who re-ceive him he
gives us life, and we give him thanks: "To you be our praise ev-er-

gain—   I   am your God;   you are my peo - ple."
made: "I   am your God;   you are my peo - ple."
says: "I   am your God;   you are my peo - ple."
more!   You are our God;   we are your peo - ple."

Words and Music: David A. Hoekema, 1978 © 1985 CRC Publications, 2850 Kalamazoo Avenue Southeast, Grand Rapids, MI 49560 [www.crcpublications.org]. All rights reserved. Used by permission.

98

We give thanks unto you

1 We give thanks un-to you, O God ___ of ___ might,
2 From of old you have led your peo - ple in faith,
3 You de-liv-ered the ones who called un - to you,
4 You have o-pened the sea and brought your peo-ple through,
5 You re-mem-ber your prom-ise age ___ to ___ age,

for your love is nev-er-end-ing;

we give thanks un-to you, the God of gods,
you have shown your com-pas-sion, strength, and love,
from ___ bond-age to free-dom, you brought them forth,
brought them in-to a land that flows with life,
you show mer-cy on those of low de-gree,

for your love is nev-er-end-ing.

Words and Music: based on *Psalm 136*, vers. Marty Haugen (b. 1950) © 1987 GIA Publications, Inc., 7404 S. Mason Ave., Chicago, IL 60638 [www.giamusic.com]. All rights reserved. Used by permission.
You must contact GIA Publications, Inc. to reproduce this selection.

Refrain

Al - le - lu - ia!___ Al - le - lu - ia! Al - le - lu - ia!

1 That Eas - ter morn, at break of day, a faith - ful wo - man
2 When Ma - ry's heart was filled with gloom as she stood weep - ing
3 "Why do you weep?" his ques - tion came? "Whose is the bo - dy
4 No long - er weep - ing, an - guish-bent, but with re - joic - ing

went her way to seek the tomb where Je - sus lay. Al-le-lu - ia!
near the tomb, a strang - er spoke, she knew not whom. Al-le-lu - ia!
you would claim?" And then, at last, he spoke her name. Al-le-lu - ia!
Ma - ry went, by Christ, the first a - pos - tle sent. Al-le-lu - ia!

Words: v. 1 Jean Tisserand (d. 1494); tr. John Mason Neal (1818-1866), alt.
V. 2-4 Delores Dufner, OSB (b. 1939) © 1994 Delores Dufner (admin. GIA Publications, Inc., 7404 S. Mason Ave., Chicago, IL 60638 [www.giamusic.com].) All rights reserved. Used by permission.
Music: *O filii et filiae*, melody from *Airs sur les hymnes sacrez, odes et noëls*, 1623; acc. Carl Haywood (b. 1949)
© Carl Haywood. All rights reserved. Used by permission.
You must contact GIA Publications, Inc. to reproduce verses 2- 4 of these words.
You must contact Carl Haywood to reproduce this arrangement.

1 Christ has a - ris - en, al - le - lu - ia.
2 For three long days the grave did its worst
3 The an - gel said to them, "Do not fear.
4 "Go spread the news: he's not in the grave.
5 Christ has a - ris - en to set us free.

Re - joice and praise him, al - le - lu - ia.
un - til its strength by God was dis - persed.
You look for Je - sus who is not here.
He has a - ris - en this world to save.
Al - le - lu - ia, to him prais - es be.

For our re - deem - er burst from the tomb,
He who gives life did death un - der - go,
See for your - selves the tomb is all bare.
Je - sus' re - deem - ing la - bors are done.
Je - sus is liv - ing! Let us all sing;

e - ven from death, dis - pel - ling its gloom.
and in its con - quest his might did show.
On - ly the grave cloths are ly - ing there."
E - ven the bat - tle with sin is won."
he reigns tri - um - phant, heav - en - ly king.

Music: Traditional Tanzanian.

Sing, O people

Refrain

Sing, O peo - ple, sing our God to - geth - er,

Capo 3: (D)
F

(G/D)
Bb/F

(D)
F

(Em7/A)
Gm7/C

raise your voic - es: sing al - le - lu - ia!

(D)
F

(Em7/A)
Gm7/C

(D)
F   *Last time*

last time rit.

Verses
Cantor   All

1 Sing with one an - oth - er: sing the love that gave us breath!
2 Dance the steps of beau - ty: dance the love that gave us breath!
3 Serve all those who suf - fer: serve the love that gave us breath!
4 Teach the way of Je - sus: teach the love that gave us breath!
5 Seek the chil - dren's wis - dom: seek the love that gave us breath!

(D)
F

(G)
Bb

(D)
F

(Em7/D)
Gm7/F

(A)
C

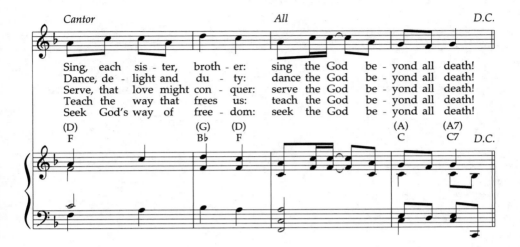

Cantor ... All ... D.C.

Sing, each sis - ter, broth - er: sing the God be - yond all death!
Dance, de - light and du - ty: dance the God be - yond all death!
Serve, that love might con - quer: serve the God be - yond all death!
Teach the way that frees us: teach the God be - yond all death!
Seek God's way of free - dom: seek the God be - yond all death!

(D)   (G) (D)   (A) (A7)
F   Bb F   C   C7   D.C.

102　The Lord, the Lord, the Lord is my shepherd

Refrain: The Lord, the Lord, the Lord is my shep-herd. The
1 You bring me rest in green, green pas - tures. You
2 My fear is gone for you are with me. Your

Lord, the Lord, the Lord is my shep - herd. The
lead me to _____ the still, still wa - ters. You
rod and staff bring com - fort sure; your

Lord, the Lord, the Lord is my shep - herd. The
guide me a - long your own right way. The
good-ness and mer - cy shall fol - low me. The

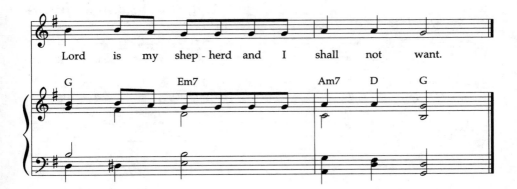

Lord is my shep-herd and I shall not want.

G   Em7   Am7   D   G

Oh, how good is Christ the Lord
Oh, qué bueno es Jesús

103

Oh, how good is Christ the Lord! On the cross he died for me.
Oh, qué bue - no es Je - sús. Que por mí mu - rió en la cruz.

He has par - doned all my sin, Glo - ry be to Je - sus.
Mis pe - ca - dos per - do - nó. A su nom - bre glo - ria.

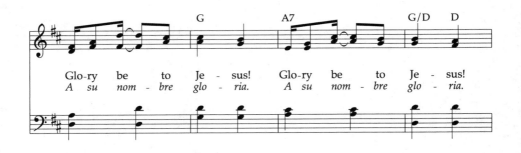

Glo - ry be to Je - sus! Glo - ry be to Je - sus!
A su nom - bre glo - ria. A su nom - bre glo - ria.

In three days he rose a - gain. Glo - ry be to Je - sus.
En tres días re - su - ci - tó. A su nom - bre glo - ria.

Words and Music: Puerto Rican Folk Hymn; harm. Dale Grotenhuis, 1985 © 1987 CRC Publications, 2850 Kalamazoo Avenue Southeast, Grand Rapids, MI 49560 [www.crcpublications.org]. All rights reserved. Used by permission.

You are my shepherd

104

Refrain

You are my shep-herd, you are my friend. I want to fol-low you al - ways,_____ just to fol-low my friend. friend.

Capo I: (D) (Em7/D) (D) (A) (Bm) (F#m/A)
Eb Fm7/Eb Eb Bb Cm Gm/Bb

1.–4. To verses | Final ending

(Gmaj7) (D) (Bm) (Gmaj7) (A) (D)
Abmaj7 Eb Cm Abmaj7 Bb Eb

Verses
Cantor

D.C.

1 I have all I need. You are my shep-herd, your hand is with me.
2 When path-ways are dark, you are there guid-ing me, keep-ing me safe.
3 You give me to eat. You make me wel-come, you fill me with joy.
4 Your good-ness I know. Your love will be with me all of my life.

(D) (Dmaj7) (Bm) (D) (G)
Eb Ebmaj7 Cm Eb Ab

D.C.

We are all children of the Lord

106

Verses
Cantor

1 To the God who can - not die:
To the God of the op - pressed:
2 For the dream I have to - day: I say
To come to love my en - e - mies: *Di - go*
3 Like that of Job, un - ceas - ing - ly:
Like that of Da - vid in a song:

Capo 3: (C)   (C/B)   (Am)   (Em/G)
Eb   Eb/D   Cm   Gm/Bb

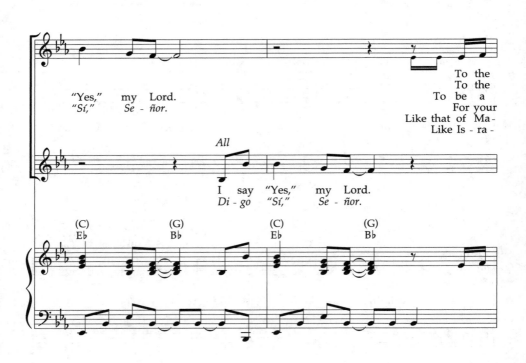

"Yes," my Lord.   To be a   To the
"Sí," Se - ñor.   For your   To the
Like that of Ma -
Like Is - ra -

All

I say "Yes," my Lord.
Di - go "Sí," Se - ñor.

(C)   (G)   (C)   (G)
Eb   Bb   Eb   Bb

One   who   hears ___ me ___ cry: ___
God   of   all ___ jus - tice: ___
heal - er   of ___ all ___ pain: ___
peace   in   all ___ the ___ world: ___
ri - a   whole-heart - ed - ly: ___
el,   for   you ___ I   long: ___

                                                                           I   say
Di - go

(C)   (C/B)   (Am)   (Em/G)
Eb   Eb /D   Cm   Gm/Bb

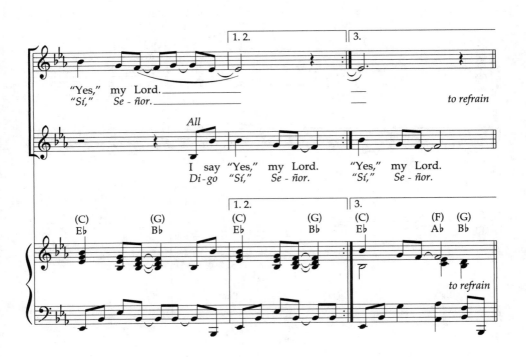

1. 2.   **3.**

"Yes,"   my   Lord. _____   ___
"Sí,"   Se - ñor. _____   ___   *to refrain*

All

I   say   "Yes,"   my   Lord.   "Yes,"   my   Lord.
Di - go   "Sí,"   Se - ñor.   "Sí,"   Se - ñor.

(C)   (G)   (C)   (G)   (C)   (F)   (G)
Eb   Bb   Eb   Bb   Eb   Ab   Bb

                                                                      to refrain

Refrain

I say "Yes," my Lord, in
Di - go "Sí," Se - ñor, en

(C) (G/B) (Dm) (G)
E♭ B♭/D Fm B♭

all the good times, through all the bad times,
tiem - pos mal - os, en tiem - pos bue - nos,

(Dm) (Gm) (C) (Em) (F) (G)
Fm B♭ E♭ Gm A♭ B♭

I say "Yes," my Lord to
Di - go "Sí," Se - ñor a

(C) (G/B) (Dm) (G)
E♭ B♭/D Fm B♭

ev - 'ry word you speak.
to - do lo que ha - blas.

107 Soplo de Dios viviente *Breath of the living God*

1 So - plo de Dios vi - vien - te que en el prin - ci - pio cu - bris - te el a - gua;
2 So - plo de Dios vi - vien - te por quien el ver - bo se hi - zo car - ne,

1 Breath of the liv - ing God, who in the be - gin - ning moved o'er the wa - ters,
2 Breath of the liv - ing God, whose e - ter - nal Word came to dwell a - mong us,

So - plo de Dios vi - vien - te que fe - cun - das - te la cre - a - ción.
So - plo de Dios vi - vien - te que re - no - vas - te la cre - a - ción.

Breath of the liv - ing God, by whom all cre - a - tion was first con - ceived:
Breath of the liv - ing God, by whom all cre - a - tion has been re - newed:

Estribillo (Refrain)

¡Ven hoy a nues - tras vi - das, in - fún - de - nos tus do - nes,
Come now and live with - in___ us, come, let your gifts en - rich___ us,

So - plo de Dios vi - vien - te, oh San-to Es - pí - ri - tu Cre - a - dor!
Breath of the liv - ing God, our Cre - a - tor Spir - it, e - ter - nal Source.

Come, Holy Spirit, descend on us

Come, Ho - ly Spi - rit, de - scend on us, de -

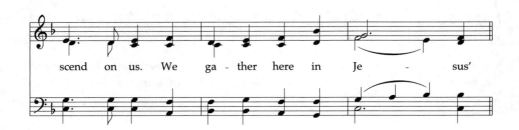

scend on us. We ga - ther here in Je - sus'

(Cantor, except last time)

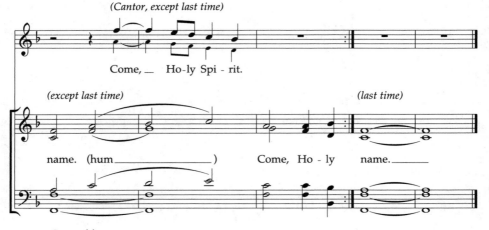

Come, __ Ho - ly Spi - rit.

(except last time)   (last time)

name. (hum_____)   Come, Ho - ly   name._____

Cantor(s):
1 Come, Holy Spirit.
2 Come, Breath of Heaven,
3 Come, Word of Mercy,
4 Come, Fire of Judgement,
5 Come, Great Creator,
6 Come to unite us.
7 Come to disturb us.
8 Come to inspire us.
(other invocations ad lib.)

I am the church

109

Refrain

I am the church! You are the church!

We are the church to - geth - er! All who fol-low Je - sus,

all a - round the world, yes, we're the church to - geth - er!

1 The church is not a build-ing, the church is not a stee-ple, the
2 We're man - y kinds of peo - ple with man - y kinds of fac - es, all

Repeat refrain

church is not a rest - ing place; the church is a peo - ple!
col - ors and all a - ges too, from all times and plac - es.

Words and Music: Richard Avery and Donald Marsh © 1972 Hope Publishing Co., 380 S. Main Pl., Carol Stream, IL 60188 [www.hopepublishing.com].
All rights reserved. Used by permission.

She sits like a bird

1 She sits like a bird,
2 wings o - ver earth,
3 dan - ces in fire,
4 is the Spi - rit,

brood-ing on the wa - ters, hover-ing on the cha - os of the
rest - ing where she wish-es, light - ing close at hand or soar-ing
start - ling her spec - ta - tors, wak - ing tongues of ec - sta - sy where
one with God in es - sence, gift - ed by the Sav - iour in e -

world's first day; she sighs and she sings,
through the skies; she nests in the womb,
dumb - ness reigned; she weans and in - spires
ter - nal love; she is the key

moth-er - ing   cre - a - tion,   wait-ing   to   give   birth   to   all   the
wel - com - ing   each won - der,   nour-ish - ing   po - ten - tial   hid - den
all   whose hearts are   o - pen,   nor   can   she   be   cap - tured, si - lenced
o - pen - ing   the   scrip - tures,   en - e - my   of   ap - a - thy   and

Gmaj7   Cmaj7   Fmaj7   Am7

Word will   say.   2   She
to   our   eyes.   3   She
or   re - strained.   4   For she
heaven-ly   dove.

B   Em   Bm7   Em   Bm7   *Last time*   E

Loving Spirit

1 Lov - ing Spir - it, lov - ing Spir - it, you have cho - sen
2 Like a moth - er, you en - fold me, hold my life with -
3 Like a fa - ther you pro - tect me. Teach me the dis -
4 Friend and lov - er, in your close - ness I am known and
5 Lov - ing Spir - it, lov - ing Spir - it, you have cho - sen

me to be; you have drawn me
in your own. Feed me with your
cern - ing eye. Hoist me up up -
held and blest: in your prom - ise
me to be; you have drawn me

to your won - der, you have set your sign on me.
ver - y bod - y, form me of your flesh and bone.
on your shoul - der, let me see the world from high.
is my com - fort, in you pres - ence I may rest.
to your won - der, you have set your sign on me.

Words: Shirley Erena Murray (b. 1931) © 1987 The Hymn Society (admin. Hope Publishing Co., 380 S. Main Place, arol Stream, IL 60188 [www.hope-publishing.com].) All rights reserved. Used by permission.
Music: Fiona Vidal-White © 2004 Fiona Vidal-White. All rights reserved. Used by permission.
Arr. John L. Hooker (b. 1944) © 2005 John L. Hooker. All rights reserved. Used by permission.
You must contact Hope Publishing to reproduce these words.

May your loving spirit

1 May your lov-ing spi-rit, be in us, with us, a-
2 May your lov-ing spi-rit, sur-round us, shield us,__
3 May your lov-ing spi-rit, hold us, help us,__

round__ us, may your lov-ing spi - rit.
shel-ter us, may your lov-ing spi - rit.
heal__ us, may your lov-ing spi - rit,

come to us, O Lord God.
come to us, O Lord God.
come to us, O Lord God.

Clap your hands

1 Clap your hands, all you peo - ple; shout un - to God with a
2 Clap your hands, all you peo - ple; Christ has as - cend - ed

voice of tri - umph! Clap your hands, all you peo - ple;
in - to hea - ven! Clap your hands, all you peo - ple;

shout un - to God with a voice of praise! Ho - san - na! Ho -
Christ has as - cend - ed with shouts of joy! Ho - san - na! Ho -

san - na! Shout un - to God with a voice of tri - umph!
san - na! Christ has as - cend - ed in - to hea - ven!

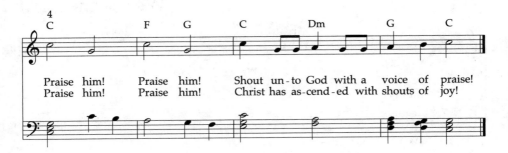

Praise him! Praise him! Shout un-to God with a voice of praise!
Praise him! Praise him! Christ has as-cend-ed with shouts of joy!

Words: st. 1, *Psalm 47:1*, par. Jimmy Owens, 1972; st. 2, Bert Polman, 1991.
Music: Jimmy Owens, 1972; harm. Charlotte Larsen, 1991. Words and Music © 1972, Bud John Songs, Inc. (ASCAP)
(admin. EMI Christian Music Publishing, PO Box 5085, Brentwood, TN 37024-5085). All rights reserved. Used by permission.

We see the Lord

Opt. descant

We see Je - sus.

Melody

We see the Lord. We see the

E

We see Je - sus. High,

Lord, and he is high and lift - ed up, and his

B7

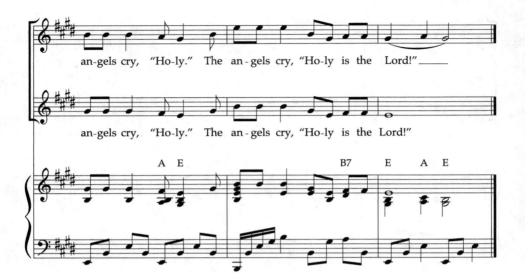

Loving Creator

115

1 Lov-ing Cre-a-tor, grant to your child-ren mer-cy and bless-ing, songs ne-ver ceas-ing, grace to in-vite us, peace to un-ite us___ Lov-ing Cre-a-tor, par-ent and God.___

2 Je-sus Re-deem-er help us re-mem-ber your pain and pas-sion, your re-sur-rec-tion, your call to fol-low, your love to-mor-row___ Je-sus Re-dee-mer, our friend and Lord.___

3 Spi-rit des-cend-ing, your light un-end-ing, brings hope and heal-ing, is truth re-veal-ing. (hum) Dis-pel our blind-ness, in-spire our kind-ness— Spi-rit des-cend-ing, Spi-rit a-dored.

(hum)
(hum)
(hum)

Spi-rit a-dored.
Spi-rit a-dored.
Spi-rit a-dored.

Words: D.T. Niles.

Music: *Halad*, Elena G. Maquiso. Words and Music © Christian Conference of Asia. All rights reserved. Used by permission.
Music: arr. © 1991 WGRG The Iona Community (Scotland) (admin. GIA Publications, Inc., 7404 South Mason Ave., Chicago, IL 60638 [www.giamusic.com].) All rights reserved. Used by permission.
You must contact GIA Publications, Inc. to reproduce this arrangement.

In the night, in the day

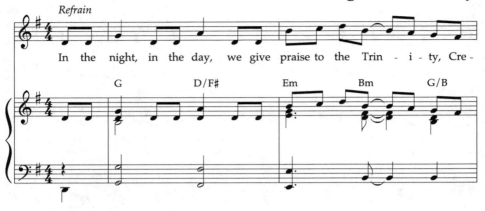

Refrain

In the night, in the day, we give praise to the Trin - i - ty, Cre-

G   D/F#   Em   Bm   G/B

a - tor, Re - deem - er, Sus - tain-er of life,   sing-ing

C   G/B   G   Am7   D

praise, liv - ing praise, breath-ing praise to our God   of glo - ry,

G   D/F#   Em   Bm

al - le - lu - ia_____ for - ev - er, al - le - lu -

ia!

To verses | *Final ending*

Verses

1–3 Blest are you, God of all Cre-a - tion, through your good-ness

we have life; / bod - y, mind and voice, spi - rit too, re - joice, / work of field and vine, now our bread and wine,

Cmaj7 Am7 Dsus4 D   C/D   D   D/C   G/B   Am

voic - es re - sound-ing in praise. / sing-ing re - news all our days. / gift of the har - vest we bring.

G   C   Am7/D   D

D.C.

Words and Music: Rob Glover (b. 1950) © 1999 Choristers Guild, 2834 West Kingsley Road, Garland, TX 75041-2498 [www.choristersguild.org].
All rights reserved. Used by permission.

Glory to God

Glo - ry   to   God;   Praise to   the   Son;

Glo - ry   to   God;   Praise to   the

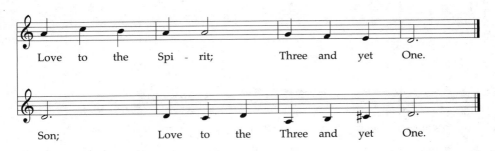

Love   to   the   Spi - rit;   Three   and   yet   One.

Son;   Love   to   the   Three   and   yet   One.

We sing of the saints

1 We sing of the saints filled with Spir - it and grace, blest
2 *(Optional verse for saint's day)*
3 We, too, have been cho - sen to fol - low the way of

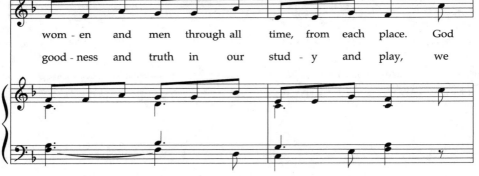

wom - en and men through all time, from each place. God
good - ness and truth in our stud - y and play, we

chose them, the ho - ly, the hum - ble, the wise to
raise up our song, liv - ing saints here be - low, with

spread the Good News of sal - va - tion in Christ.
heav - en - ly saints, as our praise ev - er flows.

Optional Verses for Saint's Days

2 **Feasts of Mary**
A lowly, young woman God's mother would be,
the first true believing disciple was she.
From cradle to cross, she would follow her Son
and share in the life everlasting he won.

Feasts of Joseph
A carpenter, upright and faithful, was called
to care for young Jesus, a child weak and small.
To teach and to guide, to embrace him in love,
reminding him here of the Father above.

Feasts of John the Baptist
A prophet and herald who made straight the way
for Jesus to come, bringing mercy's new day.
He preached to the people to change and repent,
preparing them as the Messiah was sent.

St. Michael and All Angels (September 29)
Of Gabriel, Raphael, Michael we sing,
God's messengers; joyful, glad tidings they bring;
protecting the Church, and announcing the time
when Christ shall return in his glory sublime.

Francis of Assisi (October 4)
Saint Francis was born a rich, noble young man,
but God had in mind a much different plan;
so Francis left status and money behind,
to help many people God's true will to find.

All Saints (November 1)
There are many saints whom we don't know by name,
for God works through people who never find fame.
But, gathered together, they now sing God's might,
with martyrs and prophets, in heavenly light.

All Faithful Departed (November 2)
We honor the mem'ry of those now at rest,
who followed the Gospel, whose lives were so blest;
from fam'lies and friendships, they make heaven seem
more home-like for us, in our prayers and our dreams.

Words: Alan J. Hommerding (b. 1956).
Music: *Zie Ginds komt de Stoomboot*, Traditional Dutch Melody, acc. Karl A. Pölm-Faudré.
Words and Music © 1994 World Library Publications, Inc., 3708 River Rd., Franklin Park, IL 60131-2158 [www.wlpmusic.com].
All rights reserved. Used by permission.

119

Child of blessing, child of promise

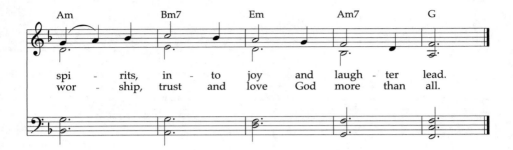

spi - rits, in - to joy and laugh - ter lead.
wor - ship, trust and love God more than all.

I am the light of the world

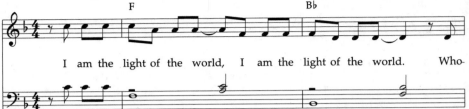

I am the light of the world, I am the light of the world. Who-

ev - er fol-lows me___ will nev-er walk in the dark, will nev-er

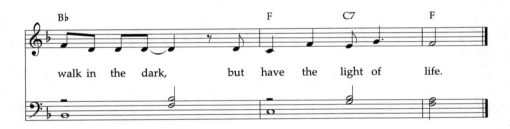

walk in the dark, but have the light of life.

Words: *John 8:12.*
Music: June Fischer Armstrong © 1991 CRC Publications, 2850 Kalamazoo Avenue Southeast, Grand Rapids, MI 49560 [www.crcpublications.org].

We bring our children

1 We bring our chil-dren, Lord, to - day as
2 On their be - half and in their name our
3 Help us in all our ways to show these

once they did in Ga - li - lee, em -
own com - mit - ment we re - new with
grow - ing souls your truth and grace, till

brace them with your love, we pray, and
them we die to sin and shame, with
they shall come them - selves to know the

1. 2.
bless each home and fam - i - ly.
them we live a - gain in you.

3.
beau - ty of our Fa - ther's face.

You have put on Christ

f play detached *no rit.*

Cantor

You have put on Christ, in him you have been bap - tized.

Al - le - lu - ia, al - le - lu - ia.

You have put on Christ, in him you have been bap - tized.

Al - le - lu - ia, al - le - lu - ia.

God, when I came into this life

123

1 God, when I came in - to this life, you called me by my__ name; to - day I come, com - mit my - self, re - spond-ing to your claim.
2 You give me free - dom__ to be - lieve; to - day I make my__ choice, and to the wor - ship of the church I add my learn - ing voice.
3 In all the ten - sions__ of my life, be - tween my faith and__ doubt, let your great Spi - rit give me hope, sus - tain me, lead me out.
4 So help me in my__ un - be - lief and let my life be__ true: feet firm - ly plant - ed on the earth, my sights set high on you.

Words: Fred Kaan (b. 1929) © 1979 The Hymn Society (admin. Hope Publishing Co., 380 S. Main Pl., Carol Stream, IL 60188 [www.hopepublishing. com].) All rights reserved. Used by permission.
Music: *Dunlap's Creek*, Freeman Lewis, arr. Margaret W. Mealy © Margaret W. Mealy. All rights reserved. Used by permission.
You must contact Hope Publishing to reproduce these words.

Great work has God begun in you

124

1 Great work has God be-gun in you, so let the Spi-rit
2 In love, God calls you to this day, and gives you strength, these
3 A-round God's ta-ble cel-e-brate the end of bond-age,
4 Great work has God be-gun in you; take on God's love in

fol-low through; the mark of Christ up-on your brow, bap-
vows to say; take up the faith that you were shown, and
sin, and hate: a feast of love and vic-to-ry, the
all you do, and may that love in you in-crease— now,

tis-mal touch re-mem-ber now.
grow, as-sured you are God's own.
gift of Christ who sets us free.
with God's bless-ing, go in peace.

In love you summon

In love you sum-mon, in love I fol-low, liv-ing to-day for

your to-mor-row. Christ to re-lease me, Christ to en-

fold me, Christ to re-strain me, Christ to up-hold me.

From my birth

1 From my birth, from my birth, you have known me, O Lord, from my birth. Before I thought or planned, my life was in your hand; you have known me, O Lord, from my birth.

2 Ev-ery-where, ev-ery-where, you pur-sue me, O Lord, ev-ery-where. Unsleep-ing day and night, nor bound by depth or height, you pur-sue me, O Lord, ev-ery-where.

3 Still you call, still you call, though I wan-der, O Lord, still you call. When wild and proud I roam, your love in-vites me home; though I wan-der, O Lord, still you call.

4 In-to life, in-to life, you will lead me, O Lord, in-to life. Through death's dark shad-ow passed, to see your face at last, you will lead me, O Lord, in-to life.

Words: Carl P. Daw, Jr., alt. © 1996 Hope Publishing Co., 380 S. Main Pl., Carol Stream, IL 60188 [www.hopepublishing.com]. All rights reserved.
Used by permission.
Harm. David Ashley White © David Ashley White. All rights reserved. Used by permission.
You must contact Hope Publishing Co. to reproduce these words.

127   One more step along the world I go

1 One more step a-long the world I go, one more step a-long the
2 Round the cor-ner of the world I turn, more and more a-bout the
3 As I tra-vel through the bad and good, keep me tra-vel-ling the
4 Give me cour-age when the world is rough, keep me lov-ing though the
5 You are old-er than the world can be, you are young-er than the

world I go; from the old things to the new
world I learn; all the new things that I see
way I should; where I see no way to go
world is tough; leap and sing in all I do,
life in me; ev-er old and ev-er new,

keep me tra-vel-ing a-long with you:
you'll be look-ing at a-long with me:
you'll be tell-ing me the way, I know: and it's from the old I
keep me tra-vel-ing a-long with you:
keep me tra-vel-ing a-long with you:

tra-vel to the new; keep me tra-vel-ing a-long with you.

Words and Music: Southcote, Sydney Carter © Oxford University Press/Church of Scotland, 198 Madison Ave., New York, NY 10016-4314 [www.oup.com/us].
u must contact GIA Publications, Inc. to reproduce these words .

Many and great

128

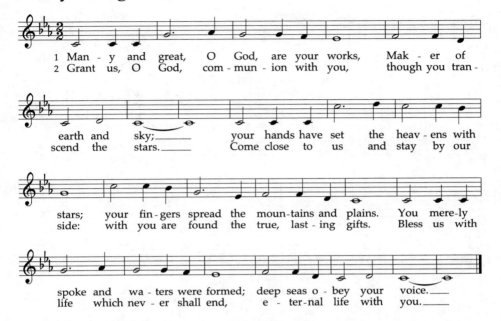

1 Man - y and great, O God, are your works, Mak - er of
earth and sky;___ your hands have set the heav - ens with
stars; your fin - gers spread the moun-tains and plains. You mere - ly
spoke and wa - ters were formed; deep seas o - bey your voice.___

2 Grant us, O God, com - mun - ion with you, though you tran -
scend the stars.___ Come close to us and stay by our
side: with you are found the true, last - ing gifts. Bless us with
life which nev - er shall end, e - ter - nal life with you.___

God of the sparrow God of the whale

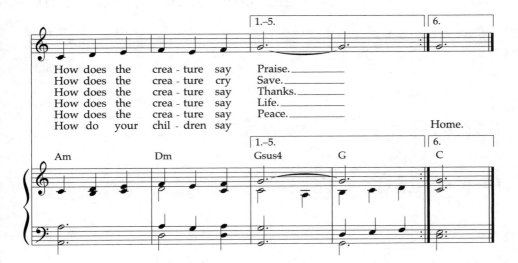

How does the crea - ture say Praise._____
How does the crea - ture cry Save._____
How does the crea - ture say Thanks._____
How does the crea - ture say Life._____
How does the crea - ture say Peace._____
How do your chil - dren say Home.

Am   Dm   Gsus4   G   C

Words: Jaroslav J. Vajda (b. 1919) © 1983 Concordia Publishing House, 3558 South Jefferson Ave., St. Louis, MO [www.cph.org]. All rights reserved.
Used by permission.
Music: *Roeder*, Carl F. Schalk (b. 1929) © 1983 GIA Publications, Inc., 7404 South Mason Ave., Chicago, IL 60638
[www.giamusic.com]. All rights reserved. Used by permission.
You must contact Concordia Publishing House to reproduce these words.
You must contact GIA Publications, Inc. to reproduce this music.

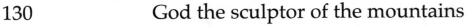

God the
(God the)
(God the)
(God the)

sculp - tor	of the	moun - tains,	God the	mil - ler	of the
nui - sance	to the	Pha - raoh,	God the	cleav - er	of the
un - ex -	pect-ed	in - fant,	God the	calm, de -	ter - mined
dress - er	of the	vine - yard,	God the	plant - er	of the

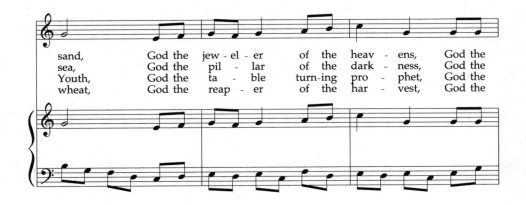

sand,	God the	jew - el - er	of the	heav - ens,	God the
sea,	God the	pil - lar	of the	dark - ness,	God the
Youth,	God the	ta - ble	turn-ing pro -	phet,	God the
wheat,	God the	reap - er	of the	har - vest,	God the

pot - ter of the land:_____ you are womb of all cre -
bea - con of the free:_____ you are gate of all de -
res - ur - rect - ed Truth:_____ you are pres - ent ev - ery
source of all we eat:_____ you are host at ev - ery

a - tion, we are form - less; shape_____ us now.____
liv' - rance, we are sight - less; lead_____ us now.____
mo - ment, we are search - ing; meet_____ us now.____
ta - ble, we are hun - gry; feed_____ us now.____

1. 2. 3.   4.

_____   God the
_____   God the
_____   God the

We are a part of all creation

Verses

1 We are a part of all cre - a - tion,
2 We are a part of ev - 'ry per-son,
3 We are a part of God's cre - a - tion,
4 We are a part of all cre - a - tion

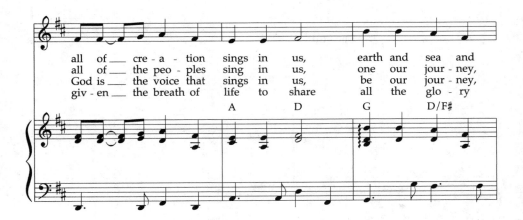

all of ___ cre - a - tion sings in us, earth and sea and
all of ___ the peo - ples sing in us, one our jour - ney,
God is ___ the voice that sings in us, be our jour - ney,
giv - en ___ the breath of life to share all the glo - ry

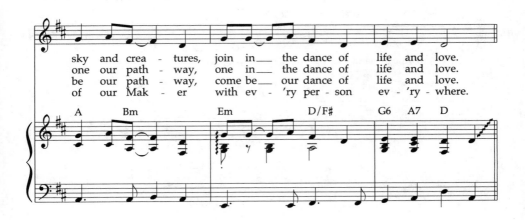

sky and crea - tures, join in__ the dance of life and love.
one our path - way, one in__ the dance of life and love.
be our path - way, come be__ our dance of life and love.
of our Mak - er with ev - 'ry per - son ev - 'ry - where.

A   Bm   Em   D/F#   G6 A7 D

Refrain

All of__ cre - a - tion, one o - ha - na,* All of__ cre - a - tion

D   G   D

sings in you;   Ma - ny__ the voic - es, one great mu - sic,

A   Bm   Em7   D/F#   G   Bm

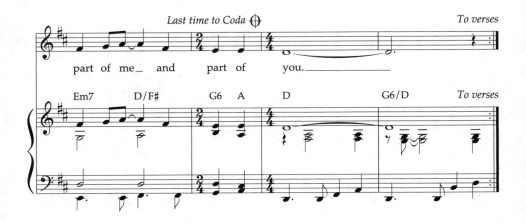

* ohana = great family

Praise to God

132

133

Heaven and earth

Cantor alone, 1st time, 2nd time Sopranos join

Hea-ven and earth, join to wor-ship your Cre-a-tor!

Women

Hea-ven and earth, join to wor-ship your Cre-a-tor!

Men

Hea-ven and earth, join to wor - ship

Sing to the Lord, praise the One from whom you came.

Sing to the Lord from the One from whom you came.

Sing to the Lord from whom you came.

Cantor first, then all

Sing a new song to the God who goes be-fore us,

Sing a new song to the God who goes be-fore us,
God be - fore us,

Hum

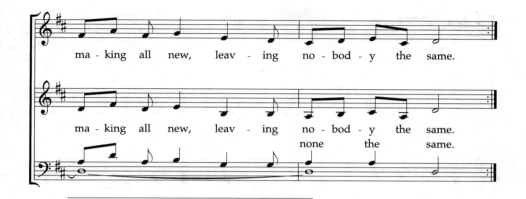

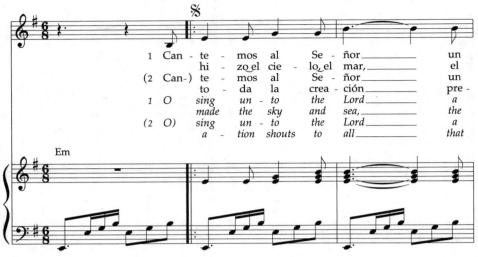

1 Can - te - mos al Se - ñor_____ un
    hi - zo el cie - lo, el mar,_____ el
(2 Can-) te - mos al Se - ñor_____ un
    to - da la crea - ción_____ pre -

1 O sing un - to the Lord_____ a
    made the sky and sea,_____ the
(2 O) sing un - to the Lord_____ a
    a - tion shouts to all_____ that

him - no de a - le - gri - a,_____ un can - ti - co de a -
sol y las es - tre - llas;_____ y vio en e - llos bon -
him - no de a - la - ban - za_____ que ex - pre - se nues - tro a -
go - na su gran - de - za,_____ a - sí nues - tro can -

hymn of cel - e - bra - tion;   O sing a song of
sun and stars of heav - en_____ and saw that they were
hymn of joy and prais - ing;_____ a song that shares our
God is grand and glo - rious;_____ and so we sing our

1. to Estribillo **2.**

mor_____ al na - cer el nue - vo dí - a;_____ El be - llas.____
dad,_____ pues sus o - bras e - ran mor,_____ nues-tra fe y nues-tra es - pe - ran-za:_____ Hoy
tar_____ va a - nun - cian - do su be lle - za.____
love,_____ ev - 'ry day a new cre - a - tion;____ God
good;_____ all cre - a - tion sings in splen-dor:____
love,_____ our faith and hope - ful wait-ing.____ Cre -
song_____ to the God of grace and beau - ty:_____

1. Em to Estribillo Em **2.**

Estribillo / Refrain

A - le - lu - ya!____ A - le - lu - ya!____ Can-
Al - le - lu - ia!____ Al - le - lu - ia!____ O

D C B7

1.

te - mos al Se - ñor._____ A - le - lu - ya!_____
sing un - to the Lord._____ Al - le - lu - ia._____

Am Em B7 Em

1.

lu - ya!   2 Can - lu - ya!_____

lu - ia.   2 O lu - ia._____

Words: based on *Genesis 1; Psalm 19:1;* Carlos Rosas, 1976, tr. C. Michael Hawn.
Music: Carlos Rosas, 1976, arr. Arturo Gonzalez.
Spanish text and melody © 1976 Resource Publications, Inc., 160 E. Virginia St. #290, San Jose, CA 95112-5876 [www.rpinet.com]. All rights reserved.
Used by permission.
Tr. and arr. © 1999 Choristers Guild, 2834 West Kingsley Rd., Garland, TX 75041-2498 [www.choristersguild.org]. All rights reserved. Used by permission.
You must contact Resource Publications, Inc. to reprint this Spanish text or melody.

Praise God for this holy ground

135

1 Praise God for this ho-ly ground, place and peo-ple
2 Praise God in whose word we find food for bo-dy,
3 Praise God who through Christ makes known all are loved and
4 Praise God's Spi-rit who be-friends, rais-es hum-bles,
5 Though praise ends, praise is be-gun where God's will is

sight and sound.
soul and mind.
called God's own.   Ha-le-lu-jah!   Ha-le-lu-jah!
breaks and mends.
glad-ly done.

Ha-le-lu-jah! God's good-ness is e-ter -

nal. _____

last time

Ped.

Words and Music: *Hemonystraat*, John L. Bell (b. 1949) © 2002 WGRG The Iona Community (Scotland) (admin. GIA Publications, Inc., 7404 S. Mason Ave., Chicago, IL 60638 [www.giamusic.com].) All rights reserved. Used by permission.
You must contact GIA Publications, Inc. to reproduce this selection.

Taste and see

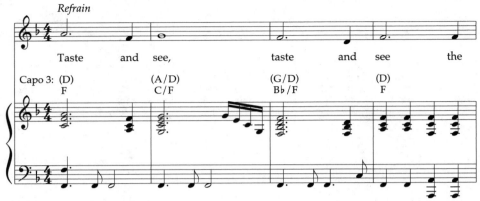

Refrain

Taste and see, taste and see the

Capo 3: (D) (A/D) (G/D) (D)
F C/F Bb/F F

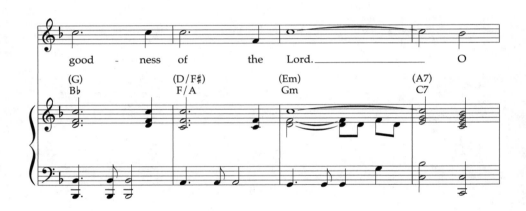

good - ness of the Lord. O

(G) (D/F♯) (Em) (A7)
Bb F/A Gm C7

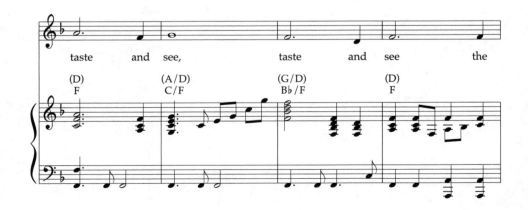

taste and see, taste and see the

(D) (A/D) (G/D) (D)
F C/F Bb/F F

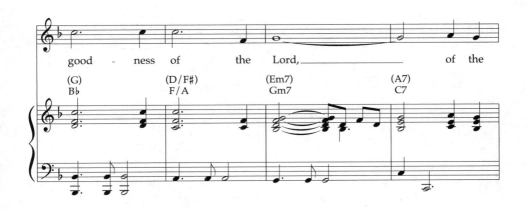

good - ness of the Lord,_____ of the

(G) (D/F♯) (Em7) (A7)
B♭   F/A   Gm7   C7

To verses   *Last time*

Lord.   Lord.

(D)   (G/D)   (D)   (Asus4) (A7) (D)
F   B♭/F   F   Csus4   C7   F

Verses
                                    ⌐ 3 ⌐

1 I will bless the Lord___ at all times._____
2 Glo-ri-fy the Lord___ with me._____   To -
3 Wor-ship the Lord,___ all you peo-ple._____

(D)   (F♯m7)   (Gmaj7)   (D/F♯)
F   Am7   B♭maj7   F/A

Praise shall al - ways be on my lips;_____ my
geth-er let us all praise God's name._____ I
You'll want for noth-ing if you ask._____

(Em7) (D/F#) (A7sus4) (A7)
Gm7 F/A C7sus4 C7

soul_____ shall glo-ry in the Lord_____ for
called_____ the Lord who an - swered me;_____ from
Taste_____ and see that the Lord is good;_____ in

(D) (F#7) (F#/A#) (Bm) (Bm7/A)
F A7 A/C# Dm Dm7/C

D.C.

God_____ has been so good to me._____
all_____ my trou-bles I was set free._____
God_____ we need put all our trust._____

(Gadd9) (D/F#) (Em) (A7)
Bbadd9 F/A Gm C7 D.C.

We thank God

We thank God for giv-ing us life,* giv-ing us life, giv-ing us life.

We thank God for giv-ing us life; we thank God to - day.

Refrain

On this day and ev - ery day, ev - ery day, ev - ery day;

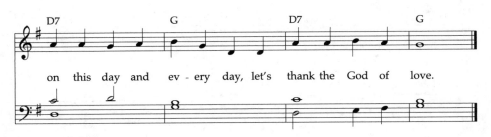

on this day and ev - ery day, let's thank the God of love.

* *Additional stanzas: love, faith, hope, joy, Mom, Dad, and so on.*

Words and Music: Kathleen Hart Brumm © 1988 in *Sixteen Scripture Songs for Small Singers*, Brummhart Publishing Co., 1708 Blooming Grove Dr.,
Rensselear, NY 12144 [www.hometown.aol.com/khbising2].

O give thanks to the Lord

Cantor

1 O give thanks to the Lord who is good,
2 Who a - lone has wrought mar - vel - ous works,
3 It was God who made the great lights,
4 God let Is - rael in - her - it their land,
5 It was God who saved us from our foes,

All

For God's stead - fast love en - dures for - ev - er.

For God's love en - dures for - ev - er.

Cantor

O give thanks to the God of gods.
God in wis - dom made the skies,
The sun to rule in the day,
On those ser - vants their land God be - stowed,
God gives food to all liv - ing things,

All

For God's stead - fast love en - dures for - ev - er.

For God's love en - dures for - ev - er.

Cantor

O give thanks to the Lord of lords.
Who fixed the earth firm - ly on the seas.
The moon and stars in the night.
God re - mem - bered us in our dis - tress.
To the God of heav'n give thanks.

For God's stead-fast love en - dures for - ev - er.

For God's love en - dures for - ev - er.

Words: based on *Psalm 136:1-9, 21-26*; adapt. I-to Loh (b. 1936), alt. C. Michael Hawn © C. Michael Hawn. All rights reserved. Used by permission.
Music: *Mihamek*, Song of Amis Tribe, Taiwan, transcr. I-to Loh (b. 1936) © I-to Loh. All rights reserved. Used by permission.

139

Thank you for the gift of Jesus

1 Thank you for the gift of Je - sus: for his
2 Thanks for all the men and wom - en who, with
3 Hopes and dreams that live a - mong us, new com -
4 Boun - teous God, take tal - ents, mem - ories, all we

life a - mong the poor, for his free - ing
o - pened hearts and ears, heard his call and
pas - sions, deep - er cares, grow from seeds of
have and dear - ly hold; work in them your

words and spi - rit, faith and hope that still en - dure,
lived his pas - sion in their strug - gles, joys, and tears.
your own plant - ing, stem from faith of our fore - bears.
pres - ent pur - pose, give them back a hun - dred - fold.

for   the   love   he   felt   and   nur - tured   in   the
Through their touch - ing,   speak - ing, teach - ing,   plen - teous
So   the   past   re -   news   the   pres - ent,   soon   the
So   your peo - ple   born to - mor - row   may with

shamed   and   dis - pos - sessed.   Through his love   our
gifts   and   guid - ing   prayers,   you   have raised in
seed   be - comes the   tree,   soon your for - est
joy   sing   out   one   day,   "God   is good and

hearts are o - pened,   through his life   our   lives are blessed.
us   the   prom - ise: we   shall be   your friends and heirs!
stretch - es high - er,   fur - ther than the   eye can see.
God   is   gra - cious,   God   has blessed us   on   our way."

1 When in our mu - sic God is glo - ri -
2 How of - ten, mak - ing mu - sic, we have
3 So has the Church, in lit - ur - gy and
4 And did not Je - sus sing a psalm that
5 Let ev - ery in - stru - ment be tuned for

fied, and ad - o - ra - tion leaves no
found a new di - men - sion in the
song, in faith and love, through cen - tu -
night when ut - most e - vil strove a -
praise! Let all re - joice who have a

room   for   pride,   it   is   as
world   of   sound,   as   wor - ship
ries   of   wrong,   borne wit - ness
gainst the   Light?   Then let   us
voice   to   raise!   And may God

F   Cmaj7   Am7/D   D   G/B

though the whole cre - a -   tion   cried:
moved us   to   a   more   pro -   found
to   the   truth in ev -   ery   tongue: Al - le - lu -
sing, for whom he won   the   fight:
give   us faith   to sing   al -   ways:

Am7   Em7   A7

Mother hen

141

1 Moth-er hen, moth - er hen, guards her ba - bies with her wings,
2 Moth-er bear, moth - er bear, guards her ba - bies with a growl,
3 Ea - gle mom spreads her wings, keeps her ba - bies free from harm,
4 Moth-ers all show their love like our God in heaven a - bove,

Moth - er hen, moth - er hen, God is like a___ moth-er hen.
Moth - er bear, moth - er bear, God is like a___ moth-er bear.
Ea - gle mom spreads her wings, God is like an___ ea - gle mom.
Thank you, God, for the care of lov - ing moth-ers_ ev - ery - where.

Mothering God

Descant

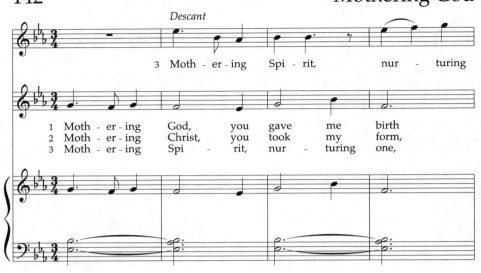

3 Moth-er-ing Spi - rit, nur - turing

1 Moth - er - ing God, you gave me birth
2 Moth - er - ing Christ, you took my form,
3 Moth - er - ing Spi - rit, nur - turing one,

one, _____ in arms of pa - tience hold me

in the bright morn - ing of this world. Cre -
of - fer - ing me your food of light, the
in arms of pa - tience hold me close, so

close,   in faith I root and grow

a - tor,   source of ev - 'ry breath,
grain___ of life,   and grape___ of love,
that___ in faith   I root___ and grow

___ un - til I flow'r, un - til I

you are my rain,   my wind,___ my sun.___
your ve - ry bo - dy for___ my peace.___
un - til I flow'r,   un - til___ I (know.)___

know._____ Moth - er -ing God_____ Moth - er -ing God.

know._____ Moth - er -ing God.

Everywhere I go

143

1 Ev - ery - where I go, the Lord is near me.
2 In the dark of night should things a - larm me,
3 In the com - ing days of joy or sad - ness,
4 Ev - ery - where I go, the Lord is near me.

If I call up - on him, he will hear me.
ev - er in his sight, no ill may harm me.
I will praise his name with songs of glad - ness.
If I call up - on him, he will hear me.

Nev - er will I fear, for the Lord is near, ev - ery - where I
I will be of cheer, for the Lord is near, ev - ery - where I
For to me it's clear that the Lord is near, ev - ery - where I
Nev - er will I fear, for the Lord is near, ev - ery - where I

1.–3.

go.

4.

go.

Words and Music: Natalie Sleeth, arr. Charlotte Larsen © 1992 Choristers Guild, 2834 West Kingsley Road, Garland, TX 75041-2498.

One, two, three, Jesus loves me

One, two, three, Je - sus loves me. One, two,

Je - sus loves you. 1 Three, four, he loves you more

than you've ev - er been loved be - fore. 2 Five, six, seven, we're

go-ing to heav'n. Eight, nine, it's tru-ly di-vine.

3 Nine, ten, it's time to end; but in-stead we'll

sing it a-gain. there's no time to sing it a-gain.

145   In you our hearts find rest

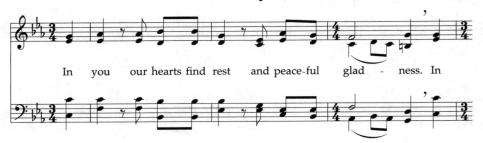

In you our hearts find rest and peace-ful glad - ness. In

you our hearts find rest and peace-ful glad - ness.

Words: *Psalm 62.*
Music: Jacques Berthier © by Les Presses de Taizé (France) (admin. GIA Publications, Inc., 7404 S. Mason Ave., Chicago, IL 60638 [www.giamusic.com].)   All rights reserved. Used by permission.
You must contact GIA Publications, Inc. to reproduce this music.

God to enfold you

God to en-fold you, Christ to up-hold you,

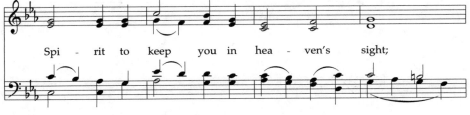

Spi - rit to keep you in hea - ven's sight;

so may God grace you, heal and em - brace you,

lead you through dark - ness in - to the light.

Oh, the love of my Lord

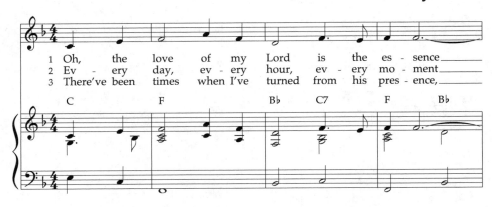

1 Oh, the love of my Lord is the es - sence____
2 Ev - ery day, ev - ery hour, ev - ery mo - ment____
3 There've been times when I've turned from his pres - ence,____

C   F   Bb   C7   F   Bb

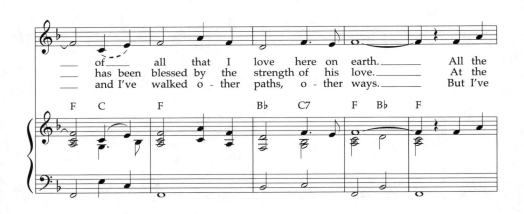

____ of____ all that I love here on earth.____ All the
____ has been blessed by the strength of his love.____ At the
____ and I've walked o - ther paths, o - ther ways.____ But I've

F   C   F   Bb   C7   F   Bb   F

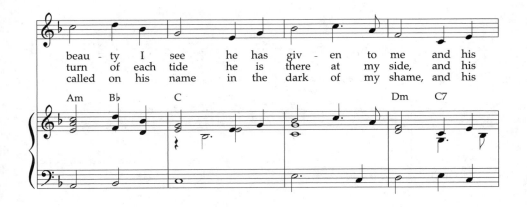

beau - ty I see he has giv - en to me and his
turn of each tide he is there at my side, and his
called on his name in the dark of my shame, and his

Am   Bb   C   Dm   C7

giv - ing is gen - tle as si - lence._____
touch is as gen - tle as si - lence._____
mer - cy was gen - tle as si - lence._____

148   Lord, my soul is thirsting

Lord, my soul is thirst-ing for a bless-ing to-day, __

Lord, my soul's a - thirst

let your pre-sence come from a - bove; come, I pray, to rend the heav-ens;

let thy pre-sence come, rend the heav'ns, come

and then come down; let your spir-it fall all a - round. __

down; let thy spi - rit fall.

Lord, my soul is thirst-ing and I want a re - fresh - ing;

Lord, I thirst.

Lord, my soul is thirst-ing and I need a fresh touch.

Touch me a - new,

Additional verses ad libitum:
Lord, my soul is thirsting for a cleansing today.
. . . for your spirit today.
. . . for your healing today.

The tree of life

1 The tree of life my soul hath seen, la -
2 His beau - ty doth all things ex - cel: by
3 For hap - pi - ness I long have sought, and
4 I'm wear - y with my form - er toil, here
5 This fruit doth make my soul to thrive, it

den with fruit and al - ways green. The
faith I know but ne'er___ can tell the
plea - sure dear - ly I___ have bought: I
I will sit and rest___ a - while: un -
keeps my dy - ing faith___ a - live; which

trees of na - ture fruit - less be, com -
glo - ry which I now ____ can see in
missed of all: but now ____ I see 'tis
der the shad - ow I ____ will be of
makes my soul in haste ____ to be with

pared with Christ, the ap - ple tree.
Je - sus Christ, the ap - ple tree.
found in Christ, the ap - ple tree.
Je - sus Christ, the ap - ple tree.
Je - sus Christ, the ap - ple tree.

Peace among earth's peoples

1 Peace a - mong earth's peo - ples_____ is like a star
2 Wars are caused by want - ing_____ what is not ours.
3 Cov - et - ous - ly plot - ting,_____ we do not pray,
4 From our war - ring sens - es_____ we seek re - lease;
5 Peace a - mong earth's peo - ples_____ is like that star

beam - ing just a - bove us,_____ so near, so far.
Why must we keep flaunt - ing_____ our law - less powers?
ask - ing our Pro - vid - er_____ to light our way.
then all earth - ly con - flicts_____ might al - so cease.
lead - ing to a man - ger,_____ so near, so far.

Though out of grasp, we long to clasp it:
We act in lust rath - er than trust that
Is it not greed rath - er than need that
Can we not share one com - mon prayer with
Some saw the light; some were in fright, but

peace a - mong earth's peo - ples,_____ so near, so far.
God who an - swers want - ing_____ will an - swer ours.
tempts us in - to plot - ting_____ when we should pray.
all of this earth's peo - ples_____ to know world peace?
all for peace were long - ing,_____ just as we are.

Let there be peace on earth

Let there be peace on earth and let it be -
Let peace be - gin with me, let this be the

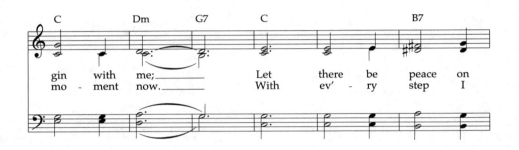

gin with me;_____ Let there be peace on
mo - ment now._____ With ev' - ry step I

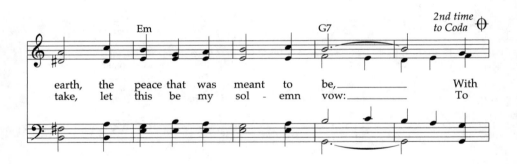

earth, the peace that was meant to be,_____ With
take, let this be my sol - emn vow:_____ To

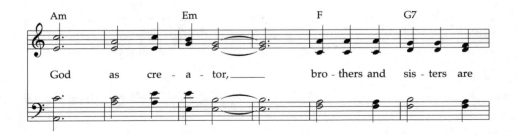

God as cre - a - tor,_____ bro - thers and sis - ters are

Peace before us

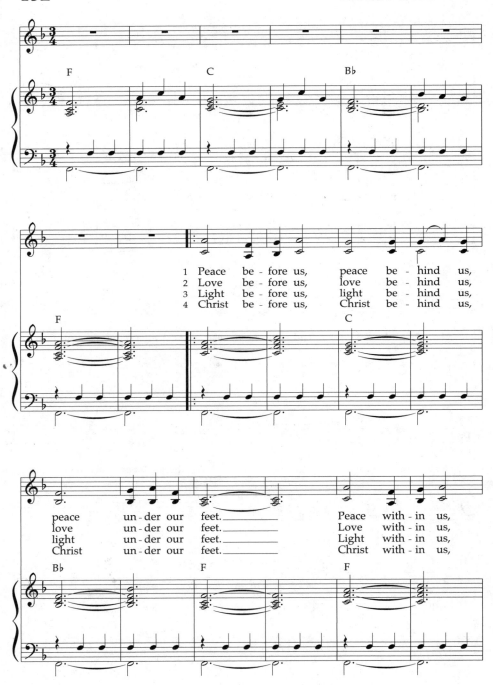

1 Peace be-fore us, peace be-hind us,
2 Love be-fore us, love be-hind us,
3 Light be-fore us, light be-hind us,
4 Christ be-fore us, Christ be-hind us,

peace un-der our feet._____ Peace with-in us,
love un-der our feet._____ Love with-in us,
light un-der our feet._____ Light with-in us,
Christ un-der our feet._____ Christ with-in us,

Let all a - round us be peace._____

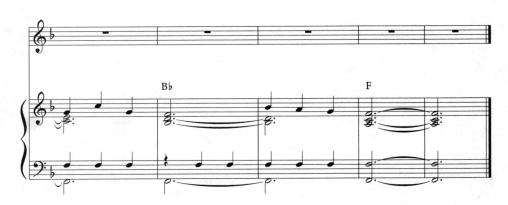

5 Alleluia, alleluia, alleluia.
   Alleluia, alleluia, alleluia.

6 Peace before us, peace behind us,
   peace under our feet.
   Peace within us, peace over us,
   let all around us be peace. *(three times)*

What does the Lord require of you?   153

1 What does the Lord re-quire of you?

2 Jus - tice, kind - ness,

3 To seek jus-tice, and love kind-ness,

Repeat ad lib.   Last time

What does the Lord re-quire of you? you?

walk hum-bly with your God. God.

and walk hum-bly with your God. God.

154

Santo *Holy*

♩ = 108–120

Estribillo / Refrain

San-to,   san - to, san - to,   san - to,   san - to,   san - to es nues - tro   Dios,
   san - to, san - to,   san - to,   san - to,   san - to es nues - tro   Dios,

Ho - ly,   ho - ly, ho - ly,   ho - ly,   ho - ly,   ho - ly   is   our   God.
   ho - ly, ho - ly,   ho - ly,   ho - ly,   ho - ly   is   our   God.

Se - ñor   de   to - da   la   tie - rra,   san - to,   san - to es nues - tro
Se - ñor   de   to - da   la his - to - ria,   san - to,   san - to es nues - tro

You are   Lord   of   all   the   na - tions,   ho - ly,   ho - ly   is   our
You are   Lord   of   all   of   his - t'ry,   ho - ly,   ho - ly   is   our

			Estrofas / Verses
1. F	2. F	F7	

Dios.   San - to,   Dios.   Que_a-com - pa - ña_a nues - tro
                                       Ben - di - tos los que_en su

God.   Ho - ly,   God.   The Com - pan - ion of our
*   Bless - ed be those who in*

Bb	C	F

pue - blo,   que   vi - ve_en nues - tras lu - chas; del
nom - bre   el   e - van - ge - lio_a - nun - cian, la

peo - ple   who   lives with us in strug - gles; Cre -
God's name   de -   clare the right - eous Gos - pel, good

		1.	2. to the beginning
	C	F	F

u - ni - ver - so_en-te - ro   el   ú - ni - co Se - ñor.
bue - na_y gran no - ti - cia de   la li - be - ra -   ción.

a - tor of the cos - mos, the   on - ly Son of God.
news of God's sal - va - tion and lib - er - at - ing   hope.

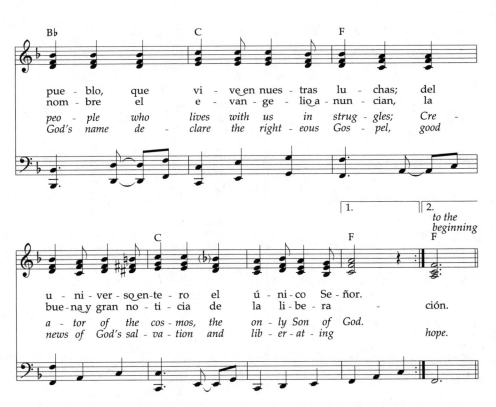

Words: Guillermo Cuéllar, tr. C. Michael Hawn.
Music: Guillermo Cuéllar, arr. Raquel Mora Martinez © 1988 GIA Publications, Inc., 7404 South Mason Ave., Chicago, IL 60638 [www.giamusic.com].

155

Come now, you blessed

Capo 1: (A)

1 "Come now, you bless - ed, eat at my ta - ble,"
2 When did we see you hun - gry or thirs - ty?
3 "When you gave bread to the earth's hun - gry chil - dren,
4 Christ, when we see you out on life's road - ways,

said Je - sus Christ to the right - eous a - bove.
When were you home - less, a strang - er a - lone?
when you gave shel - ter to war's ref - u - gees.
look - ing to us in the fac - es of need,

"When I was hun - gry, thirs - ty, and home - less,
When did we see you sick or in pris - on?
When you re - mem - bered those most for - got - ten,
then may we know you, wel - come and show you

sick and in pris - on, you showed me your love."
What have we done that you call us your own?
you cared for me in the small - est of these."
love that is faith - ful in word and in deed.

Words: Ruth Duck © 1979, 1992 GIA Publications, Inc., 7404 S. Mason Ave., Chicago, IL 60638 [www.giamusic.com].)
All rights reserved. Used by permission.
Music: Emily R. Brink © 1994 CRC Publications, 2850 Kalamazoo Avenue Southeast, Grand Rapids, MI 49560. All rights reserved. Used by permission.
You must contact GIA Publications, Inc. to reproduce these words.

Bendice, Señor, nuestro pan

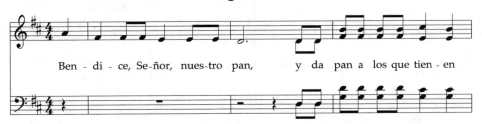

Ben - di - ce, Se-ñor, nues-tro pan, y da pan a los que tien - en

ham - bre y ham-bre de jus - ti - cia a los que tien - en

pan. Ben - di - ce, Se - ñor, nues-tro pan.

Translation
May the blessing of God be on our bread and
give bread to those who are hungry;
and a hunger for justice to those who are fed.

Words: Anonymous, Spanish, tr. Daniel Viggiani © Daniel Viggiani. All rights reserved. Used by permission.
Music: Federico Pagura, arr. John L. Bell (b. 1949) © 1997 WGRG The Iona Community (Scotland) (admin. GIA Publications, Inc., 7404 S. Mason Ave.,
Chicago, IL 60638 [www.giamusic.com].) All rights reserved. Used by permission.
You must contact GIA Publications, Inc. to reproduce this music.

157 Oh, come, Lord Jesus

1 Oh, come, Lord Je-sus, be our guest, and let your gifts to
2 Oh, come, Lord Je-sus, be our guest, and let your gifts to

us be blest. Oh, may there be a good-ly share on
us be blest. Come deep with-in our hearts to dwell, that

ev-'ry ta-ble ev-'ry - where.
we may all your good-ness tell.

* May be sung as a round.

Words: Traditional Table Prayer, adapt. Susan Briehl, reprinted from *Come, Lord Jesus* © 1996 Augsburg Fortress, PO Box 1209, Minneapolis, MN 55440-1209 [www.augsburgfortress.org]. All rights reserved. Used by permission.
Music: Thomas Tallis; arr. Donald Busarow, from *All Praise to You Eternal God* © 1980 Augsburg Fortress, PO Box 1209, Minneapolis, MN 55440-1209 [www.augsburgfortress.org]. All rights reserved. Used by permission.

All night, all day

158

All___ night, all___ day, an-gels watch-ing o-ver me, my Lord.

All___ night, all___ day, an-gels watch-ing o-ver me.

1 Now I lay me down to sleep. An-gels watch-ing o-ver me, my Lord.
2 Lord, stay with me through the night.

Repeat refrain

Pray the Lord my soul to keep. An-gels watch-ing o-ver me.
Wake me with the morn-ing light.

Now it is evening

1 Now it is eve - ning: lights of the cit - y
2 Now it is eve - ning: lit - tle ones sleep - ing
3 Now it is eve - ning: food on the ta - ble
4 Now it is eve - ning: here in our meet - ing

G   D/F#   C/G   G

bid us re - mem - ber Christ is our Light.
bid us re - mem - ber Christ is our Peace.
bids us re - mem - ber Christ is our Life.
may we re - mem - ber Christ is our Friend.

Am7   G/B   C   Dsus4   D

Man - y are lone - ly, who will be neigh-bor?
Some are ne - glect - ed, who will be neigh-bor?
Man - y are hun - gry, who will be neigh-bor?
Some may be stran - gers, who will be neigh-bor?

Bm   Em   Am   Dsus4 D

Where there is car - ing Christ is our Light.
Where there is car - ing Christ is our Peace.
Where there is shar - ing Christ is our Life.
Where there's a wel - come Christ is our Friend.

COPYRIGHTS

OneLicense.net
7343 S. Mason Avenue
Chicago IL 60638
1-800-663-1501
1-708-458-5900
Fax 1-708-458-4940
www.onelicense.net

Christian Copyright Licensing Int'l.
17201 NE Sacramento Street
Portland OR 97230
1-800-234-2446
1-503-257-2230
Fax 1-503-257-2244
www.ccli.com

Abingdon Press - see *T.C.C.*

Amity Music Corp.
1475 Gaylord Terr.
Teaneck, NJ 07666
201-833-4808
(F) 201-833-4808

Augsburg Fortress
PO Box 1209
Minneapolis, MN 55440-1209
www.augsburgfortress.org
800-421-0239
(f) 800-722-7766

Birdwing Music (ASCAP) - see *E.M.I.*

Boosey & Hawkes, Inc.
35 E. 21st St.
New York, NY 10010
www.boosey.com
212-358-5350

Brummhart Publishing Co.
1708 Blooming Grove Dr.
Rensselear, NY 12144
 www.hometown.aol.com/khbising2
518-286-1837

Bud John Songs – see *EMI*

Celebration
PO Box 309
Aliquippa, PA 15001
www.communityofcelebration.com
724-375-1510
(f) 724-375-1138

Choristers Guild
2834 West Kingsley Rd.
Garland, TX 75041-2498
www.choristersguild.org
972-271-1521
(f) 972-840-3113

Christian Conference of Asia
96 Pak Tin Village Area 2
Mei Tin Road, Shatin NT
Hong Kong SAR, CHINA
www.cca.org.hk/info/infoframe.htm

Church of Scotland, The – see Oxford

Concordia Publishing House
3558 S. Jefferson Ave.
St. Louis, MO 63118-3968
www.cph.org
314-268-1000

Copyright Company, The – see T.C.C.

CRC Publications
2850 Kalamazoo Ave. SE
Grand Rapids, MI 49560
www.crcpublications.org
616-224-0819

Desert Flower Music
PO Box 1476
Carmichael, CA 95809
www.strathdee_music.com

E.M.I. Christian Music Publishing
PO Box 5085
Brentwood, TN 37024-5085

GIA Publications, Inc.
7404 S. Mason Ave.
Chicago, IL 60638
www.giamusic.com
800-442-1358 x 56
(f) 708-496-3828

Hal Leonard Corp.
PO Box 13819
Milwaukee, WI 53213
www.halleonard.com

Harvestcross Productions
258 School La.
Springfield, PA 19064

Hinshaw Music, Inc.
PO Box 470
Chapel Hill, NC 27514
www.hinshawmusic.com
919-933-1691
919-967-3399

Hope Publishing Co.
380 S. Main Pl.
Carol Stream, IL 60188
www.hopepublishing.com
800-323-1049
(f) 630-665-2552

Hymn Society, The – see Hope

Integrity Music
1000 Cody Rd.
Mobile, AL 36695
www.integritymusic.com
800-533-6912

Iona Community (Scotland) – see GIA

Jann-Lee Music – see MCCG

Jenkins, W.L.
– see Westminster John Knox Press

Licensing Associates
935 Broad St. #31
Bloomfield, NJ 07003
www.waltonmusic.com
919-929-1330
(f) 919-929-2232

Lumko Institute, The
PO Box 5058
Delmenville, South Africa
www.catholic-johannesburg.org.za

Malaco Music Group
PO Box 9287
Jackson, MS 29386
www.malaco.com
601-982-4522
(f) 601-982-4528

Malted Milk Music
575 Riverside Dr. # 51
New York, NY 10031-8545
212-368-7117

Mayhew, Ltd., Kevin
Buxhall, Stowmarket
Suffolk IP14 3BW, UK
www.kevinmayhew.com
01-449-737-978
01-449-737-834

Methodist Church (UK)
see Hope Publishing Co.

MCCG
145 Attorney St.
New York, NY 10002
212-473-6702
(f) 212-473-6708

OCP Publications
(Oregon Catholic Press)
5536 NE Hassalo
Portland, OR 97213
www.ocp.org
800-548-8749
(f) 800-462-7329

Oxford University Press
198 Madison Ave.
New York, NY 10016-4314
www.oup.com/us
212-726-6000

Pilgrim Press, The
700 Prospect Ave.
Cleveland, OH 44115-1100
www.thepilgrimpress.com
800-537-3394

Presses de Taizé (France), Le
see GIA Publications, Inc.

Resource Publications, Inc.
160 E. Virginia St. #290
San Jose, CA 95112-5876
www.rpinet.com
408-286-8505
(f) 408-287-8748

Savgos Music - see Malaco

Scripture in Song - see Integrity Music

Selah Publishing Co.
4143 Brownsville Rd., Suite 2
Pittsburgh, PA 15227-3306
www.selahpub.com
800-852-6172
(f) 412-886-1022

Stainer & Bell Ltd. - see Hope

Taizé (France), Le Presses - see GIA

T.C.C. - The Copyright Co.
1026 16th Ave. South
Nashville, TN 37212
www.thecopyrightco.com
615-321-1096

United Church Press
Cleveland, OH
www.unitedchurchpress.com

United Methodist Publishing House
see T.C.C. - The Copyright Co.

Walton Music -
see Licensing Associates

Westminster John Knox Press
100 Witherspoon St.
Louisville, KY 40202-1396
www.ppcbooks.com
800-227-2872
(f) 800-541-5113

WGRG (Wild Goose Resource Group)
see GIA Publications, Inc.

Word of God Music see T.C.C.

World Council of Churches
475 Riverside Dr.
New York, NY 10027

World Library Publications, Inc.
3708 River Rd.
Franklin Park, IL 60131-2158
www.wlpmusic.com
800-566-6150
(f) 888-957-3291

TOPICAL INDEX

INDEX OF FIRST LINES

First lines are in regular typeface. The second language of the first line is in *italic*. Popular titles are in **bold**.

INDEX OF TUNE NAMES

INDEX OF AUTHORS, TRANSLATORS, SOURCES

INDEX OF COMPOSERS, ARRANGERS, SOURCES